T0064540

Making Sense of Numbers and Math

My Method for Learning

Dr. Cary N. Schneider

authorHOUSE®

AuthorHouse™
1663 Liberty Drive
Bloomington, IN 47403
www.authorhouse.com
Phone: 1 (800) 839-8640

Published by AuthorHouse   07/24/2015

ISBN: 978-1-5049-2288-3 (sc)
ISBN: 978-1-5049-2287-6 (e)

Print information available on the last page.

Any people depicted in stock imagery provided by Thinkstock are models, and such images are being used for illustrative purposes only. Certain stock imagery © Thinkstock.

This book is printed on acid-free paper.

TABLE OF CONTENTS

CHAPTER 1

Introduction

Why I wrote this book:

You might wonder why I would write this book. I am not a math teacher, mathemetician, physicist, or considered a math expert. I had never thought about writing a book about math or learning math. I am a physician and prior pharmacist and therefore, have had a lot of experience in math and science. I was always very good at math and numbers, but never thought that I had any unique talents. I always have had a method for looking at and thinking about numbers and doing math, but never thought that it might be unique. I also never thought to even discuss my method with anyone through out my entire life.

However, when I shared my thoughts and vision about numbers and math to others, I realized that I might have a unique perspective. I personally don't claim to have a special or unique perspective or knowledge; however, others have told me that I do. This comes from several certified teachers and math instructors. After I write this, it is possible that I might find out that it is more common than what I believe it to be. Yet, at the time of this writing, and through the research that I did, I have yet to see any quite like it.

Therefore, I decided to tell my story, methods, and philosphy as a non expert, and hope this will help at least a handful of children and maybe adults to be better at math and numbers. My basic premise is that these different methods can be taught and learned. If this helps only a handful of parents and their children and maybe others, then I have accomplished my goal. If nothing else, maybe a book (and accompanying game) by a "non-expert" will give a different point of view and initiate some further dialogue.

There is a significant problem with a lack of math knowledge and skills in this country. I don't have special knowledge of what the exact problem is or what to do about it, nor did I want to do an extensive amount of research on the subject. There is probably already enough said and written about that. I have no doubt that teachers and math educators everywhere are doing an outstanding job of educating our children. I am sure they have much more knowledge than me about proper teaching methods.

Instead, at the end of the book (Appendix C), I included some research I did perform on a wide range of areas of "math education". I include some textbooks on the latest research and how to take that research and apply it to the classroom. It includes reference to YouTube videos that provide a good approach to math education. And it includes a study that documents improvements in math and numbers skills after playing "number board games". This supports the use of my accompanying game that I invented: ***Nelson's Train Stops: A Numbers and Math Game***. Appendix B will explain what this game is all about and how it uses my philosophies for the child to play and learn.

So, instead of this being a comprehensive book on math education, I want to share with you, the reader, what I know about numbers and math, and my approach and philosophy to math and numbers. I hope then that others will find value in my approach. Parents and their children might be able to utilize my methods and improve their math knowledge and skills. In fact, I wonder if even older children, teens, and young adults who have always struggled with math, might find this helpful.

Not being in the eduational field, it is possible that there is a similar book and philosophy already published. However, when I have discussed my approach with many different certified teachers, they were surprised, and felt that my methods were unique enough to warrant taking it to the public. Also, with the moderate amount of research I did do for this book, I still have not seen anything written that is exactly like this type of approach or concept.

My Background:

I thought it would be helpful or at least interesting to let you know what my background is and what gives me ANY credibility in writing a book on numbers and math. Even though I did not get a degree in mathematics, physics, statistics, or teaching mathematics, I did have a career that involved lots of numbers and lots of mathematics. Maybe because I was not formally trained in a mathematics career, I had to develop my own perspectives and this made me better.

I grew up in a small town, Savannah Missouri. Even in a small town, we found lots of things to do. We grew up playing lots of sports, but when the whether was bad; we would play lots of board and card games. The board games were mostly the numbers types of games, so we were playing with and using numbers frequently. I believe that this is what initiated my approach to numbers and math that I discuss below, and the basis of my accompanying game (***Nelson's Train Stops***).

At Savannah High School, (Savannah, Missouri) I studied math and science which included all of the available math classes. At that time (1970s) there weren't official honors classes. In spite of that, I did take plenty of math classes. In high school, I took Algebra, Geometry, Algebra II, and then a class called "Mathanalysis", which would be considered Pre-calculus today. I also took Chemistry, Biology, and Physics. I was always good at math and always understood math and math problems. I always thought that numbers were part of life and fun and logical. I also realize now, that I had my own way of thinking about numbers and math, but, I didn't realize that it may have been unique.

I then went on to College (University of Missouri), and I declared myself a "pre-med major". I somehow tested out of college algebra in my pre-entrance examination and started in "Honors Calculus". However, after that, I decided I didn't want to take any more calculus, but continued to take several other courses involving lots of math: Chemistry, Physics, as part of my pre-med prerequisites.

I then applied and was accepted to Pharmacy School at the University of Missouri – Kansas City. There, almost all of the course work involved some mathematics. I then graduated and practiced as a hospital pharmacist for 3 years. I also used math frequently during all of this time. My background in mathematics and my approach served me well, as I never had any difficulty with the coursework.

I then decided to go on to medical school and become a physician. Again, my math background and approach served me very well during medical school, residency, and practicing as a family physician and then an emergency physician. As you might guess, I was very good at computing medication dosages. I could easily compute pediatric dosages and intravenous drips in my head, which saves lots of time during busy stressful situations.

Given all of the above, I have always felt numbers and math to come relatively easy, but also to be a part of life. I felt I had a very logical approach to numbers and therefore always made sense. This might be due to the amount of math I was exposed to, but also to my approach I learned at a very early age. Hopefully this will make you feel like I have at least enough credibility for you to read on and learn what I am talking about.

Why I wrote this book:

I commented above that I decided to write this book after talking with several teachers about my approach to numbers, and they found it unique. However, I thought I'd explain further on how I could have figured that out after all of these years.

My grandmother died in 2008 at the age of 99. Even though not quite making 100, she lived a full life with a good portion of her mental alertness up until the very end. My wife, Laura, and I drove up to St. Joseph, Missouri for the funeral. We saw many family members, my brothers, my sister, my aunt, and several cousins. We had a nice funeral and a nice visit. My brother, his wife, my sister, my wife, and I decided to meet at a local restaurant to catch up further.

We talked about many issues, and I don't even remember why, but the topic of math and numbers came up. My sister is a certified teacher, and I just happened to bring up how I approach numbers and my method for doing math. Ironically, I had not ever discussed this before. Why I brought up right then and why I hadn't brought up before is a mystery.

As I discussed what I did with math and numbers, my sister, and the others there, expressed a considerable amount of amazement. "I do math by following the numbers I see in my head", I said. They all said that they had not heard of that before, and what I see is extremely unique. I explained further how the numbers look and how I use my numbers to help me with math computations. I was especially surprised that my sister, the teacher, had not heard of anything like that. We talked about that for a short while, but we then went on to other conversations. However, after that, I began to think more about it. I then asked a few others about this concept and I got the same response. This then prompted me to begin working on the concepts. I started writing down my thoughts, started writing this book, and invented the new game: ***Nelson's Train Stops.*** (Nelson happens to be my middle name, but it was also my late father's middle name, but the name he went by. His full name was John Nelson Schneider, but his father's name was also John and therefore, he went by Nelson.)

If you wonder why it took so long to finish my projects, I actually was working full time as an adminstrative physician up until recently. I was able to retire early, and then spend time working on all of my other "projects".

Another motivation for me to write this book and the game, are my two beautiful and talented daughters, both of which did very well academically. One is a CPA accountant/ auditor and the other an attorney. As you might imagine, one was good at math and the other not so much.

As a Dad, I tutored my daughters in numbers and math. My CPA daughter was always very good at math, and when I helped her on certain occasions, she always seemed to understand what I was talking about and I was able to help. In fact, my instructions often helped her more than her own teachers did. We just seemed to click; however, my attorney daughter, not as much.

Sometimes, she would understand my instructions and it would help, but often not. I told her the same things I told my other daughter and they didn't seem to work as well. Fortunately, my older daughter seemed to be able to tutor her much better.

All of these times, I didn't realize that I had my own method of working with numbers and math. I didn't think it was different and only later did I realize that neither had my ideas and vision. I believe that if I had realized that, and been able to work with those concepts, I could have helped them more. They would have understood what I did and possibly learn from it. I wonder if this isn't happening in the classroom today.

How I become good at math and numbers:

I started playing games at a very early age. My parents were very good about playing games with my brother and me very early. We probably started as early as age 2-3. My brother was just 1 year older than me, so we did everything together. We seemed to feed off each other throughout our childhood, and that included games and sports. Once they got us started, we would spend hours playing board games and cards by ourselves. We never realized that we were establishing a pattern of math and number learning for the rest of our lives.

We played several types of board games (Candy Cane Lane, Chutes and Ladders, Careers, Life, Yahtze, Monopoly, and others.) We also played all kinds of card games. We started out playing Rummy and solitaire, then played hearts, spades, and even Poker for pennies or toothpicks. When I went to high school, we played lots of spades with friends, then later learned and started playing pinocle and bridge.

One thing my parents would do would be to casually hint how to do better at card games. Since my brother and I were so competitive, that was all we needed to try and beat each other, even though my brother would almost always win. But the things that made us very good at cards were to count cards and keep close track of what was played and what was likely left in the deck. Both of my parents were good at helping us to learn to play these games better. My father was very good at playing and counting cards, especially in poker. My mother joined a bridge club then taught us how to play.

All of this time, we didn't realize this was helping us, by establishing a pattern of numbers and math, for the rest of our lives. We just thought numbers were part of life and fun. From the beginning, we both caught onto numbers and math very easily. However, it wasn't without playing with and using numbers a lot.

Based on all of this, I believe I developed my visual at a very early age, possibly even 3 or 4 years old, and probably from playing board games. I would watch the boards themselves to a great extent and it left a visual imprint in my brain. I still remember what many of them look like. As I got older, my visual probably evolved and become more refined based on my continued life experiences.

I learned to be very visual in math and would use that imprint as kind of a map for numbers. This allowed me to always have a great perspective of numbers. I could always see what my teachers were talking about, because I could see it.

Summary:

Hopefully this will peak your interest and motivates you to continue to read the remaining book. I am not a teacher or have any special training or education in Math Education or Math Theory. However, as you can see my background as a pharmacist and physician, has given me lots of experience in working with numbers and math problems. I have some reasons o believe my approach to numbers and math is unique and maybe signiicant. Whether it will be considered a "game changer" is to be determined. I just hope it helps some children and possibly some adults.

CHAPTER 2

My Philosophy of Numbers and Math

I described above how I became good at math and came to develop my method and philosophy. There is a lot of research and information on the philosophy and best ways to learn numbers and perform math. There may be a better way that is demonstrated in all of this information. You may have your own method that is totally different and works great for you and may even be better.

I never saw any research before I developed my method, and actually developed it without even realizing it. As above, my goal is to demonstrate my method, philosophy, and techniques that I have used all of my life. Then others can utilize what is helpful to them, and possibly utilize my methods. My basic premise or belief is that my method or any method can be learned. It's just a matter of getting the information to children and even adults who need it.

My Philosophy of Numbers and Math:

One thing that you might notice is that my philosophy and methods involve a systematic approach. The goal is to think about numbers in an optimal way to learn their principles and perform math problems; then to translate all of that into a process that can be learned and used by everyone. Everyone needs a plan, method, or pattern of learning math.

I also believe everyone can learn this method. However, it is possible that my pattern would not work with everyone and another method would work much better. I believe that any child can learn how to think about numbers and use common techniques that will help them perform much better at numbers and math.

Learning early is ideal. All they need are the Tools and Processes that should improve learning and math skills. I can sum up my philosophy of, and how I approach math, into four parts:
- *Visualization*
- *Relationships & Perspectives*
- *Principles, Rules, and Skills.*
- *Repetition*

Visualization:

I realize that there are different types of "learners", and you can probably already summize that I am a visual learner. I have always learned much better when I see it, versus just hearing about it. I think most people do better once they see a visual versus only hearing a description or instruction. Therefore, the saying: "A picture is worth a thousand words", is mostly true.

Educational research may determine or has determined the best way to learn math. However, I am presenting what works best for me, and very possibly, what may work best for others.

As I was saying, even when I hear verbal instructions, I need to visualize what is being said, and that is what I remember. When I take directions, I map it out in my head. I may need instructions repeated a couple of times, but once I have visualized it, I have it locked in. If I am able to see a map, I remember it for the entire trip.

That is how I also learned numbers and math. I had a very strong visual that I used my entire life. Whenever, a teacher would talk about any numbers or math problems I would follow the visual in my head. I then would use my own personal visual pattern to compute problems (eg, 2+2=4). The visualization for numbers is the same type of map. One might try to visualize individual numbers or specific problems: (2+3=5). However, this is nothing more that strict memorization, and doesn't allow the student to have a reference or perspective, as in the next section.

You might interpret this as that I simply saw random numbers and math problems, and essentially, just memorized. This is what I believe most children are asked to do and are trying to do. I suppose that may be better than nothing, but it relies totally on memorization without giving relationships, perspectives, and ability to encorporate rules and principles. My method does not involve rote memorization of numbers and problems.

I will explain how this works for me in the next chapter. Again, it is possible that another type of visual may also work, and it is possible that this has been researched and reported on before. However, I am showing how I utilize my method for visual learning.

Relationship/ Perspectives:

Part of having a visual impression is to have it with a spatial relationship. This relationship puts numbers in some type of chronological order. It is not enough to know what numbers represent, but one needs to be able to have a perspective of where numbers fall. This warrants learning and seeing a certain pattern that leaves a permanent impression about where numbers lie. The map and perspective then allows the student to see the relationships that occur between numbers.

As above, I have a very specific pattern that I have developed at a very early age. This begins with numbers 1-10. Learning the relationships with these numbers is important. This will be used for the remainder of all numbers. Seeing the difference and distance of the multiples of 5 and 10 are also key to knowing where all of the numbers fall. Using the same relationships can be used for all. A few examples include:

o   A seven is 3 less than a 10. However, a 17 is also 3 less than 20; a 27 is 3 less than 30, and so on. Having a visual impression with proper perspective allows the student to see this relationship up to infinity.

o   Take the numbers 35 and 50. Both are multiples of 5, however what are their other multiple and what separates them? Seeing both on a map or grid automatically gives the student a perspective, that 35 is approximately 2/3 of the way to 50. The student can then quickly learn that 35 is divisible by 7 and 50 by 10, and that they are 15 apart.

Principles, Rules, and Skills:

I originally did not have this section as this could be included into the above relationships and perspectives. However, as I wrote, I realized that this is a separate section that needs attention on its own. I also have included 2 chapters that list many of these rules and principles, even though I have not included near all of them.

These principles, rules, and skills can only be applied properly, if the student has learned the above two: visualization and relationships of numbers. This is where the student actually learns how to perform math computations.

Why didn't I just call it: "Doing Math Problems"? Well, that is the goal; however, the whole process requires the student to learn rules and principles of numbers then learn skills in doing math problems. This will bring it all together and allow the student to understand and remember.

It seems that children often will learn more skills in a sport than in math and reading in school. Any child in an orgainized league, especially if in an elite sports program, will get lots of very specific instructions on "skills". Let's take baseball. They are not just told to go out and "play" baseball, without extensive and explicit instruction. To throw a ball: spread your feet, turn your shoulders, take the ball way behind your head, step toward your target, turn your shoulders, throw your ball, and follow through. That is just one skill necessary to play baseball. The same detail needs to go into learning numbers and performing math.

Repetition:

Visualization, relationships, and principles, as in any good learning method, must then be accompanied by time and repetition. There has to be repetition, so that the impressions and problems can be ingrained into the minds of young people, and to all.

I knew this before, but I especially learned this when I took freshman calculus in college. I would learn the formulas and they made perfect sense in class, however, initially, I did not put the time to do repeat the problems and work similar ones to make sure they were ingrained in my head. I then flunked my first exam and was shocked. But I used that experience for the rest of my time in college and did much better.

The trouble with this, is that how do you get students and young people to use math and numbers on a repetitive basis? It sounds like drudgery to even the most ambitious student. The idea is to find ways for students to want to do the necessary repitition that is essential to make all of this part of their lives, not just something they have to do.

Different types of games have been around for a long time. With the advent of computer games and now the common use of the smart phone and tablet, the number of game applications (apps) are even more common.

With all of that, why is there seemingly little interest in numbers and math games? I am not a teacher and I don't know what is being used or promoted by elementary and math teachers. I did a search for math and numbers games and there appears to be a huge selection. However, when I observe children playing games, I don't ever see them playing math games. I certainly don't ever see these being advertised. I only see the most violent ones being promoted.

Board games have been around for as long as I remember and probably for centuries. In general they are very simply made and very simple to play. However, they can be very thought provoking. It requires that you sit and interact with others which in turn gives you a big incentive to show what you know and then try to win the game.

As above, I played lots of board games and feel it was important part of my educational development in numbers and math. In the reseach section, you will see that Board Games have shown to improve learning of numbers and math skills for children.

I decided then to develop a new board game designed to teach children numbers and math using many of the principles and philosophies outlined in this book. ***Nelson's Train Stops*** is a new game I developed that is simple however, allows the child to begin to build his/her numbers and math memory. You might find it not too dissimilar to other board games with numbers; however, I have some of my principles built into the game itself. It also points out those principles while playing the game. I hope that children will find it fun while learning the principles outlined here. Appendix B gives you a snapshot of what the game is about.

Summary:

It is important to understand my philosophies of numbers and math: Visualization, Relationship & Perspectives, Principles, Rules, & Skills, and Repetition. All of these are necessary in order to learn, understand, and truly be good at math.

The child must visualize what they are doing, and see the relationships and perspectives of each number. Then he/she must learn the appropriate principles, rules, and skills, otherwise there might not be a connection of what they are doing. Then, he/she must repeat it over and over again. Games are a great way to learn while having fun. It is interactive which keeps the child engaged and attentive. However, that still may not be enough.

A person will only take it to the next level, and become truly proficient if they can somehow incorporate the concepts into their everyday life. In other words: Math as part of life. I believe people who are excellent at math, do that. Math could be considered another language, so that the child or student actually thinks in the numbers world.

To at least some extent, I do that today. I use any opportunity I can to use my numbers skills. When any numbers or math situation or discussion comes up, I will automatically think of my visual and use my principles of numbers and math. Given any opportunity, I revert to my numbers and math memory.

CHAPTER 3

How I Approach and Learn Math and Numbers

What I do and what I see:

Finally we get to the meat of the book and the part that prompted me to write this book. As noted in the chapter above, I utilize a visual method that does not involve strict memorization. It allows for me to visualize, while utilizing my other philosophies of seeing perspectives and relationships, utilizing rules and principles, and then using repetition so that it is a permanent imprint in your memory.

The main aspect of my technique is that whenever I think about numbers or math, I see the numbers in my head. This does not mean that I see a single random number all alone in empty spaces. When I do a math problem, I don't see a few numbers in a singular formula or even a "chart" that is often taught to children.

I have developed a map or pattern of numbers that I use; which includes all numbers. That means that my pattern is set up so that I can see any number all the way up to infinity. This might seem incredible at first; however I will elaborate and explain what I mean and how it works. Instead of "I see dead people" (Movie: *Sixth Sense*); I see numbers.

I don't know when or how I started thinking about numbers like this, but certainly as long as I can remember. Even as a young child I must have decided that I needed to have some type of reference point and pattern to give me my perspective which shows the relationship of numbers to each other. This means that math wizards and experts are probably developing their own methods, while those that struggle in math did not figure that out and/or were not taught.

I discovered that if I visualize numbers as I do math problems, then it was much easier to perform such problems and more likely to get correctly. From that, I developed a certain pattern of numbers and it has stuck with me all of my life. I don't even think I knew I was doing that, nor realized than many people don't.

I believe I developed my pattern after years of many hours of playing board games as it seems to be a hybrid of those games. My map is essentially my own personal game board and will use in my new board game: ***Nelson's Train Stops.***

I have used this map or game board for as long as I can remember, and still use today. Through the years, I was able to use and add my principles of numbers and math. My number pattern is one that has worked very well for me, because it is very logical and versatile. For simplicity sake, I will call this "My Pattern" for the remainder of the book, and I will refer to it very often. It is the basis for how I learned numbers and math,

What "My Pattern" looks like:

Figure 1 shows you the basics of what "My Pattern" looks like. The basic and main part of the map starts out with the numbers from 1 to 100. The pattern is such that I can see where a number is on the pattern. It is essentially a map of numbers. It might seem that this would be small and restrictive. However, the versitility is such that I can expand the pattern. It is actually possible for me to see any number up to infinity. It works like an expanding and contracting map when you are working with Mapquest or Google Maps. However, practically, I don't think I have had the need to see any number larger than the trillions. As you might know, this is what our current national debt is. ($18,000,000,000,000+).

Whenever I hear a number or use numbers in problems, I use my tracking device and automatically see the number or numbers on my map. I can find any number on this map. When I do problems or computations, I use my map to assist me to get the answer. For simple computations, I can use it to automatically give an answer, as the problem is already built in, especially for those under 100.

Section One to 100:

The basic pattern for "My Pattern" is the numbers one (1) to 100 (**Figure 1**), and is the initial pattern for the rest of the number spectrum. It is a winding pattern but has reasoning and logic to it. Learning all of the principles here sets the pattern for the rest of the numbers. This part of the pattern (1-100) then repeats itself to infinity.

It starts out at the bottom of the page with numbers 1 to 10 that start the pattern in larger blocks. Numbers 1 to 10 are the basis for all other numbers, and important to understand first. Learning the principles of 1 to 10 is essential to establishing rules and principles for all other numbers. Whatever happens from 1-10 are the same as what happens repeatedly up to infinity.

Starting at 11, the pattern starts to turn upwards and then winds through the pattern. But then it repeats the 1-10 pattern and rules up to 100. So, I could then see how the numbers at 81 to 90 are similar to the numbers 1-10; yet they are in a totally different area of the map. They are connected, but they are far apart. So, learning the principles of 1-10, and then expanding to the entire initial 1-100 map is essential and makes all of the other learning much easier. I have been able to use it with math rules and shortcuts. I can also add rules to my pattern, and visualize those. It makes performing computations much easier.

The most important aspect is that I had a map or pattern that gives me a visual and spacial perspective of numbers. It gives a feel for where one number compares to another. Five (5) is on the same level as a nine (9), but five (5) is a long way from 85. By simply looking at the map or have in your head, I can easily tell that subtracting 15 from 20 is going to be a smaller number than subtracting 5 from 20. Maybe intuitive, but not when you are first starting out, and a student is struggling with what numbers mean.

Just to clarify, I am currently talking about whole numbers, and not fractions or decimal numbers. I will discuss those later.

Also, if you were wondering, I started with 1 and not zero. Zero is technically not a number, but it is the starting point for all numbers, even negative numbers and fractions. So when you go to 1, you have started counting, added one (1), and started all number principles up to infinity.

You can also see a more detailed and illustrated version of my map and plan by purchasing ***Nelson's Train Stops***.

Pattern for 1 to 1 thousand (1000):

The section from 1 to 100 is the basis for the rest of "My Pattern", but as I stated above, it is only the beginning of the entire number spectrum. However, you must learn all of the principles within the initial 100 as all of these also repeat. I visualize this pattern as 10 maps of 100, end on end. You can also visualize the 1-100 Section layered on top of each other. However, I prefer not to have layers, only one continuous long road map. As you go higher, the details of the pattern look smaller and smaller, while including more and more numbers into the pattern.

Figure 2 demonstrates how the pattern/ map works and looks like up to 200. The first 100 then repeats itself to make the next 100, which takes you to 200.

Figure 3 then shows you how it would look as you go up to 400. Each box is its own section of 100 and therefore uses the exact same pattern and principles and rules as the first 100.

Figure 4 then show how the pattern looks up to 1000. Each box is a section of 100 at different levels. To visualize each section, go to **Figure 1** to see more detail of each section.

Figure 5 shows how to use "My Pattern" up to 100,000. Each space or number contains 1000 numbers. Use my original 1-100 Pattern to visualize up to 100,000.

All of the rules and principles that are learned in the first 100 are used in all of the other 100s level. So, whether you are in the 200s, 400s, or 900s, you always know where the numbers are and how to use your principles and how to do the "math" in these sections.

You don't actually have to recreate each section as a copy of the first 100 each time. You can utilize the same 100 pattern, but just remember that you are in a different 100 level. For example if you are in the 300s, then use the same pattern as in the first 100. 350 will have the same look, feel, and principles as 50, but at a different level.

So let's look at some examples and see how it works.

- 125 – Where is this number and what are the properties? Go past 100 to the 101-200 section. Find the 25 in that section and realize that you are the next section. The properties for this are the same for 25; it is an odd number, divisable by 5 and 25. You can use the rules of 5 and 25. But also, it is ¼ of 500, so a multiple of 500. By looking at 125 on the whole scale of 1-1000, you can see where it falls and get a perspective of where it is. This then will be a permanent fixation in the memory.

- 733 – Where is this number and what are the properties? Go to the 1-1000 scale (Figure 4) and find the 701-800 section, then find the 33 on the 1-100 scale. It is an odd number. It would have the same properties as 3 and 33 for addition and subtraction. However, even though it ends in a 3, it is not divisable by 3. If you add all the digits together, you get 13, which is not divisable by 3. So, it has no other rules, but, again, you can see where the 733 is in the whole map of 1-1000. If you get a credit score of 733 and find this number and see the number in your mind, I think you are certainly more likely to remember.

Pattern for 1000 to 1 million (1,000,000):

Starting at 1001, the pattern then takes a turn. This occurs every time there is a number that adds three zeros: at 1000, then at 1,000,000 (million), then 1,000,000,000 (billion) and so on. From 1000, the pattern then totally repeats itself for every 1 thousand. (**Figure 5**)

The pattern of 1-100 then repeats itself, but at a higher level. In other words, each one thousand is squeezed into each space of the original 1-100 Pattern; or the entire 1-1000 is the equivalent of one on the original pattern of 1-100.

Look at the original 1-100 Pattern. Then imagine that there are 1000 spaces or pieces squeezed into each space. However, the 1000 spaces are keeping the same shape, only much smaller. Also, each thousand spot can be imagined to be so huge that it holds the 1000 pieces or spaces. Therefore, putting 1000 into each spot in the 1-100 Pattern, then goes up to 100,000. Then if you look at the 1-1000 Pattern, and put 1000 pieces or spaces into each spot, then that would come up to 1,000,000 (one million). This last visual gives you an idea of how big a million really is: a thousand spaces with a thousand pieces or spaces fit inside each space. Let's now call this the 1000-100,000 pattern, which as above, looks just like the 1-100 pattern.

Therefore, when you are at 5 thousand, it actually looks like the original "5" on the 1-100 map, but it actually holds a thousand spaces or pieces within each number. If you are looking for a very specific number, you would then have to drill down to the next level.

Some examples:

-   3723 – You can find this number on Figure 5, as I already have all the numbers mapped out up to 5000. Find the 3000 (on the 1000-100,000 pattern); then go to the next section of 3000 to 4000; then go to the 700s level (on the 1-1000 pattern), and then with a magnifying glass find the 23. You don't have to use a magnifying glass, but you get the picture. This is exactly what you do every time. However, you won't have all of the maps or patterns laid out in front of you. You have to expand (and contract) the patterns in your mind in order to find and use your numbers.

-   9234 – Let's use a similar number not on the map: Find the 9 on the 1000-100,000 pattern; then go to the 1-1000 pattern and find the 200s level, then go back the 1-100 pattern and find the 34. However, it actually looks like what you did in the first example, and you keep all of these in perspective in your mind.

-   32,573: Find the 32 on the 1000-100,000 pattern; then go to the 1-1000 pattern and find the 500s level, and then go to the 1-100 pattern and find the 73.

-   593,617 – You'll need to see the pattern for 1000 to 1,000,000 in your mind, which looks just like the 1-1000 pattern, but with 1000 numbers in each space. Find the 500,000s level: then find 73,000 in the 1000-100,000 pattern; then the 600s level on the 1-1000 pattern, then on the 1-100 pattern – 17.

So, the pattern from 1000 to 1,000,000 looks the same as 1-1000. The map gets recreated with each one space represents or contains one complete 1000 pattern. In other words: 1000 spaces each with a map of 1000 numbers. (1000x1000). It then goes up to 1,000,000.

One Million to One Billion:

A million is a common number. Everyone wants to have a million dollars. When someone mentions a million of anything, it sounds like an incredible amount. So it helps to think and visualize what a million looks like. One million has six zero's (1,000,000) and therefore is 1000 times 1000; or you can say it is 1000 thousands.

"My Pattern" starts over once you reach 1000, and then the pattern starts all over again at 1 million. From here, look on the intial pattern of 1-100. Imagine then that there are 1 million pieces or spaces within each number. So 1=1 million, 2=2 million, 3=3 million, and so forth. You then drill down into the pattern to find and visualize a specific random number. Using the pattern of 1-100 with a million numbers in each space, then takes you to 100,000,000. In order to get up to 1 billion, you need to use the 1-1000 pattern, each with a million numbers crammed into each space. That is what it looks like. Therefore, from here, I will call it the 1 million – 1billion pattern.

Some examples include:

   o   3,789,345 – Find 3 on the 1million -100 million pattern, and imagine that is the 3 million. Then within the next million, you would use the 1000 – 1,000,000 pattern and find 789,000; then within the 1-1000 pattern, find the 300s level, and then 45 within that level but using the 1-100 pattern.

   o   123,537, 721 – Find the 100s level on the 1million to 1 billion pattern; then find the 23 million; then go to the 1000 – 1,000,000 pattern and find the 500,000s - level, and then 37,000 on the 1000 – 100,000 pattern; then on the 1-1000 patternwhich is the millions. Then within the next million, you find 537,000 on the 1 million pattern. Then within the next 1-1000 pattern, find the 700s level and then 21.

One Billion to One Trillion:

A billion is also frequently talked about. The richest people in the world have tens or hundreds of billions of dollars. One billion is the same as 1000 millions. Or, you can start counting by one million and when you reach 1000 million, you have reached 1 Billion. One billion adds another 3 zeros to 1 million, or in other words, a thousand millions. As I discussed before, this starts the whole pattern over again.

Going from 1 billion to 1 trillion, you would look at the 1-100 pattern and then imagine within each space is 1 billion numbers, spaces, or pieces.

We will then call this the 1 billion to 100 billion pattern, which then looks like the 1-100 pattern. Then once you pass 100 billion, you then go to a pattern that looks like the 1-1000 pattern, but then we would call this the 1 billion to 1 trillion pattern. This gives you a "perspective" of how big these numbers are and their relationships.

Some examples include:

- 57,632,498,721: Find the 57 billion on the 1 billion-100 billion pattern, then the 600s million level then 32 on the 1-100 million pattern; then 498 on the 500,000s level of the 1000 − 1 million pattern; then 721 on the 1-1000 pattern.

- 235,993,126,753: Find the 35 billion on the 200 billions level, of the 1 billion − 1 trillion pattern; then 993 million on the 1 million to 1 billion pattern; then 126 on the 1000-1 million pattern; then 753 on the 1-1000 pattern.

I will stop at 1 Trillion. It is the result of putting 1000 Billions together. If you go past 1 Trillion, then the pattern starts over again. Imagine having 1 Trillion pieces into each of the spaces in the original 1-100 pattern (on up to 1000). Think for a second that the National Debt of the United States is 18 Trillion dollars and growing. (http://www.usdebtclock.org/) This perspective truly tells you how incredible this is, mind boggling, and alarming.

Summary:

This is an explanation of exactly what I see and use and have used throughout my life. As you can see, it has a unique look. I am not sure how it got to look exactly like that, but I believe it is a hybrid of different board games I grew up playing and other factors.

This may seem complicated at first. However, the pattern is very simple and very logical. The beauty of this type of approach is that once it is learned and practiced, it stays with you for your entire life. It's like programming a formula into your brain that may be difficult to program, but then it automatically runs forever. It's the same thing that occurs when working with the formulas in Microsoft Excel or a computer program. It takes some time to do or figure out the program, but once put into place, it does thousands or millions of computations in an instant.

It starts with 1-100 and it quickly gives a spatial perspective of all numbers from 1 -100. The pattern continues on by repeating the 100 up to 1000. Then the entire pattern repeats itself up to 1,000,000. It then restarts, up to 1 billion, and then to 1 trillion; then on to infinity if and when that might be necessary. Look at all of the **Figures** and then compare and put them together.

By using this pattern, anyone can visualize every single number in the number spectrum up to infinity. How someone uses this visualization is up to the individual. It may require some training and education. However, this or a similar pattern, if learned, will have a life long benefit to the student or child.

This pattern satisfies three of the four points of my philosophy. It gives a visual pattern one can learn and utilize. It demonstrates perspectives and relationships. Then it allows the incorporation of rules, principles, and skills into the pattern. Then, with my game: ***Nelson's Train Stops***, (Appendix B) it then allows repetition to ingrain all of it into the permanent memory of the child/ student.

If this still seems confusing, then I will go over a few different ways to look at the pattern to help get the concept.

As I mentioned already, you can look at it like you do with Google Maps or Mapquest. You might find a country, state, or region then continue to focus down to the location you are looking for. If you are looking for a specific city or town, the Google map will take you straight to the spot. However, then, you zoom out and see what region you are looking at, then what state and maybe what country. You use the same principles in "My Pattern".

Another way to look at it is to think of a drop down menu. Drop down menus are commonly used for many different things. When you save websites, you save them to a folder, and then it is hidden until you click on the folder. Saving files on a computer will often be in a folder that is saved in another bigger folder.

In the movie the Matrix, the rebel group was frantically looking for the real "Neo", who was being artificially kept alive in a maze of "pods". They had to scan millions of "pods" in a matter of seconds to find him before they were discovered.

You can look at it as a universe of numbers, where Earth is a "one" but also part of the solar system, which is part of the galaxy, and each star is another solar system, with a multitude of galaxies. Remember the show "Cosmos" with Carl Sagan, who used to say "Billions & Billions & Billions….of stars".

However, my favorite way to think about this is from the movie "*__Animal House__*". If you happen to be a big fan of "*__Animal House__*" Movie, as I am, then you remember Donald Sutherland (Mr Jennings) and Tom Hulce (Pinto) exploring the Universe and the Micro-universe of their minds while getting very high on marijuana. Pinto said:

"That means that...our whole solar system...could be, like...one tiny atom in the fingernail of some other giant being......This is too much! ... OR.. That means...one tiny atom in my fingernail could be--Could be one little... tiny universe... Too Much!"

CHAPTER 4

Rules and Principles of Numbers

I believe it is important for any child/ student to learn and understand the basic rules and principles of numbers and each number's relationship with all of the others. The child could use this to perform computations in his/her head. However, the main goal is to give them the proper perspective and relationships with the numbers, even if they don't compute in their head.

Every number has its own special functionality, spatial relationship, and how it interacts with the other numbers. It is important to know these number principles before getting into Rules and Principles of Math, even though there is considerable overlap.

Every time you hear a number, it holds a special place within the entire spectrum of numbers.

> o   For example, think of the number 374. This is a random number. Can you visualize where this number is? Could you do so before reading this book? Are you beginning to now? This is a pretty insignificant number, but there are several things you can say about it: it is an even number; it lies within the 300's level, it is almost three fourths through the 300's, it is one less than 375, which would be more of a round number.

It is also important to learn these principles using some type of "visual" aide. That could either be "My Pattern" or a board game such as **Nelson's Train Stops**. The properties then become ingrained into the memory as you visualize and/or play a game.

I will start out with the numbers from 1-10, as the rules for these are the basis of the rules for all other numbers, as they repeat forever. Using the rules of numbers 1-10 gives you a reference point for all the other numbers. I will then review many of the other numbers that have important rules and principles. These are the numbers that I have found important to know or be aware of.

Remember that every number has its own rules and principles. You may already know or find other numbers that you find important to you, or you use as a significant reference point.

Be sure to use "My Pattern, Nelson's Train Stops, or another visual aide as you learn these rules. Then, use Nelson's or another game to "repeat" hundreds or thousands of times.

Principles of 1-10:

It is important to know the principles and rules of the numbers 1-10. These are the most important of all. They are the first 10 numbers, but also, their rules and principles are the ones that are used for the entire number spectrum. The numbers from 1 to 10 each has its own rules and principles and repeats themselves, in the same order, over and over again into infinity. Therefore, the numbers 1-10 are going to have the same or similar properties as 61-70, 101-110, 621-630 and so on. If you take 3, any number with a three at the end, are going to have similar properties. I will review each, in what I believe are the most important.

Just to clarify, numbers start at 1, because zero is not considered a real number. However, zero is the starting place for all numbers. So, in order to get to any number on a grid or map, you can add it to zero. For example, in order to get to 1, you are essentially adding 1 to 0. Also, you can say that any number added to zero, is that same number. (Eg, 0 + 635 = 635). In multiplication, any number multiplied by zero is always zero. That is because if you were to add any number of zero's together, the answer will always be zero. Therefore, we will use zero (0) as a number, whether it is technically a number or not.

One (1):

One is the most basic and important number. Every other number is divisable by 1. Adding a one is just like counting. Therefore, as you count, you are actually adding 1 each time. This may seem intuitive to most of us, but not necessarily intuitive to all and especially not to the very young child. If you add a one to any number, the answer is always the next number.

In a game such as **Nelson's Train Stops**, each "step" is also the same as adding 1. Counting twice or going 2 steps is the same as adding 1 twice or then is adding a 2.

Subtracting a 1 is the same as counting backwards. Or, subtracting a 1 from any number is the number just before. In a board game, moving a piece "back" one space is the same as subtracting a 1. A child should learn very early that counting forward and backward is the same as adding and subtracting.

Multiplying any number by 1 means that there is just one of that same number, so it equals the same number. Dividing any number by 1 means that number is divided into 1 part. In other words, it stays the same.

Now, compare the one to Zero, 5, and 10. 1 is 1 more than zero, but it is 4 spots less than 5, and 9 less than 10. Adding 5 to 1 or any other number ending in 1 will end in 6. Any number ending in 1 is also 1 more than the prior number ending in 0. If a number ends in 0, it is then divisable by 10, but I will call here a "10". Adding or subtracting 10 to any number ending in 1 will again end in 1.

I will explain this concept in the section on the Rules of 5s and 10s,

Two (2)

Two (2) is my second most important number. Adding a 2 is considered the same as "counting twice", or adding 1 twice. When you add a 2, then you skip the next number. When you subtract a 2, then you do the same in reverse.

Any number that is divisable by 2 is an EVEN number. If it is not, then it is an ODD number. If a number ends in 0, 2, 4, 6, or 8, then it is divisable by 2, and considered an EVEN number. If a number ends in 1, 3, 5, 7, or 9, then it is NOT divisable by 2 and considered an ODD number. Simply by learning these numbers as either even or odd helps tremendously in doing all computations. Adding or subtracting a 2 to or from any EVEN number will result in an EVEN number. Adding or subtracting a 2 to or from any ODD number will result in an ODD number.

Adding or subtracting a 2 should be as automatic as adding or subtracting a one or counting forward or backward. Adding a 2 to any number means it is going to the next even number, or the next odd number. Subtracting 2, is the same in reverse. Therefore, you should be looking at "My Pattern", ***Nelson's Train Stops***, or another pattern while you are reading and learning this. Look at the pattern and see where all the even and odd numbers are. Think about moving 2 spots as you go up and down the pattern.

Multiplying a 2 means that you "double" that number. Dividing by a 2 means that you "half" it or divide it in half. If you multiply any number by 2, whether it is even or odd, will result in an even number. For example: 2 (even) x 9 (odd) = 18 (even). That is because there are 2 – nines; however, then there are 9 – twos. Repeating 2s and all even numbers will always result in or land on an even number.

Therefore, multiplying any even number x another even number gives an even number. Multiplying an even number x an odd number will give an even number. Only when an odd number is multiplied by another odd number will the result be an odd number.

Ten (10):

I am jumping to 10(ten), as it is my next most important number. The rules and properties of ten are also considered in my "Rule of 10s". Ten works as a reference point for any addition and subtraction. Every 10 numbers or spaces is a number that is divisable by 10, or what I consider a "10". So when you are adding or subtracting other numbers, you can always use "a 10" to use as a reference.

Nelson's Train Stops has a "train station" for every 10 spaces. So 20, 30, 40, 50, 60, 70, 80, 90, 100 are all considered "a ten" and are marked by a "train station".

In addition and subtraction, you can always use "a ten" as the reference point. In relation to other numbers, it is important to know where all the other numbers are in relationship to 10 or a multiple of 10. How far is the number from "a ten"?

The numbers 1-9 all have a relationship with a 10. Knowing that relationship helps for all aspects of math. This can then be used for any number ending in 1-9 and where it is in relationship with a 10 or multiple of ten.

For example: 7 is 3 away from 10, but 17 is 7 more than 10, but 3 away from 20; 47 is 7 more than 40 and 3 less than 50.

Also, adding or subtracting a 10 to or from any number means that it will end in the same number as you started. Or, you can accomplish the same thing by adding (or subtracting) a 1 to the 10's column. For examples: 17+10=27; 23+10=33; 104+10=114; 17-10=7, 52-10=42.

This then shows another property of 10, in that it works like a "1" but with a 0 at the end of it. So adding a ten is the same as adding a 1 in the 10s column. For example adding a 10 to 273 would be the same as adding a 1 to the 10s column, which equals 283. Adding a 20 to 273 is same as adding a 2 to the 10s column, which equals 293. This is the case for all of the multiples of 10 (or 10s). They work the same as 1-9 but with a 0 on the end.

Multiplication and division: Ten works just like a one, but with a zero. Therefore, it uses the same principles, except in the "tens". Any number with a zero at the end is divisable by 10. Children should learn to count by 10s at an early age (I'm sure most do). So, taking any number and multiply by 10, means that you just add a 0 at the end of that number. Example is 27 x 10 equals 270. This also works in reverse if you divide any number by 10, you take a zero away. 380 divded by 10 is 38. But what if you find that the number you are dividing does not end in a 0. Well, the trick is to move the "decimal" to the left. However, that gives a decimal number, and not what I want to talk about here.

Use some type of a visual to see where the 10s are on the pattern or map. If you are on a "10", then adding or subtracting 10 means you can easily jump to the next 10. If you are on any other number, you can see exactly what the answer is.

For example: If you are currently on a 20, then adding 10, you can easily see the answer is 30, and this should be automatically seen and done. If you add 20, then you can easily see the answer is 40. I automatically see this on "My Pattern" in my mind.

The **Nelson's Train Stops** Game designates the 10's spot with a "Train Station". So, every 10 is a Train Station, and the child can see exactly the relationship of numbers with the 10's. The child can easily learn this pattern by using this game

Five (5):

Five (5) is the next most important number. I use the phrase: the "Rule of 5s". This is very similar to the "Rule of 10s". There is obviously considerable overlap between the two, as every other 5 falls on a 10. It is important to keep them separate but use both, this refers to all of the multiples of 5 (5, 10, 15, 20, 25, 30,…).

In regards to the 5 itself, it repeats itself for all numbers. Every number that ends in a 0 or a 5 is divisable by 5. Every other 5 lands on a 10, as 5 is ½ of 10. Therefore, multiplying a 5 by a 2 is 10. Also, multiplying a 5 by any even number then equals a number ending in 10, or considered a "10". If you multiply a 5 by an odd number, then the answer will end in a 5.

Children should learn to count by 5s just like counting by 10s. This will give them a reference that 5s can be identified. Using a visual aide, the child should be able to identify all the numbers that end in 5 or 10, and see these every 5 spaces, and see the spatial relationship of all of them.

When learning the other numbers, it is important to see the relationship with the closest and next 5 or 10. Every number has a relationship with a 5 or 10. How far away are you from the next 5 or 10? Knowing the distance of your spot (or any number) to the previous and next 5 or 10 helps to visualize the math question or move. The distance (numbers) between them are always the same, and gives a consistent reference point for all computations.

There are only 4 numbers or spaces between each multiple of 5; therefore, every number is always 1-4 spaces away from a multiple of 5. This will be used for addition and subtraction of the different numbers below. If you add or subtract and have to cross a 5 or 10, then you will use a "crossover" technique, and that will be reviewed below.

Adding or subtracting a 5 will always put the new number in the same relationship with the multiple of 5 as the old number. (Eg, 8 + 5= 13, 8+15= 23, etc.). This is the same principle that is used with the 10s, but with multiples of 5 instead.

Nelson's Train Stops identifies every 5 as a "train". You can see how each number is in relationship to a 5 (or 10 as above). See how adding 5 puts the next number in the same relationship as it was before with the "5s": Equal distance from the last 5 and next 5. Example: 8 plus 5: 8 is 2 less than 10 and 3 more than 5. 13 is 2 less than 15 and 3 more than 10, and therefore 13 is the answer. This is easily seen on the board.

CrossOver Technique:

I will briefly go over the "cross over technique" here, but since it is a math technique, I review it in more detail in the next chapter. I don't know if this is an official technique or if so, the proper name, as I didn't find any results with a web search. However, it is what I use as a technique, and what I call the "crossover technique". Any time you do addition or subtraction that crosses a 5 or a 10, this technique can be used. It also gives a perspective of the numbers you are working with.

It allows you to use the perspective and relationship of a number with 5 or 10 to solve the problem. If the problem crosses a multiple of 5 or 10, then you can add part of the number to come to five or 10, then use the rest of the number to add onto 5 or 10. For example: the problem 4 + 3 crosses a 5. You might memorize this problem in a chart or "math table", but what if you forget, or a similar problem is much more complicated. Let's start with 4. If you know the relationship of 4 with 5, then you know it is 1 less than 5. Start by adding 1 of the 3, which takes you to 5; then add the remaining portion (2) which then equals 7. This creates a simpler problem (5+2) which is much easier to solve as you know that 7 is 2 more than 5. Essentially you have solved a math problem without really doing any math, but by knowing relationships only.

The rules and principles of the remaining 1-10 numbers (3, 4, 6, 7, 8, and 9) are discussed below in chronological order. Remember that every number is important and has its own rules and principles that should be learned and remembered.

Three (3):

Three is 3 more than 0, is 2 less than a 5, and is 7 less than a 10. Adding a 5 causes it to be 3 more than a 5 or =8. Adding a 10 causes it to be 3 more than 10 or 13.

This means that the child can learn and remember that adding a 2 to 3 is always 5; not because they memorized the equation or a "chart", but because they will see it on a map or pattern. They just know that 3 is 2 away from a 5, or that 2 is 3 away from a 5. If a number ends in 3, then you would still use the same rules for addition and subtraction as the 3 itself.

Three is a multiple of 6 and 9. Therefore, if any number is divisable by 6 or 9, it is also divisable by 3. Therefore, using some of the rules of 6s and 9s can be used for 3. However, just because a number ends in 3 does not mean it is divisable by 3. If you add all the digits of the number together and the sum is divisable by 3, then the number itself is divisable by 3. This is the same rule that can be used for the number 9. (If the digits added are either 9 or divisable by 9, then the whole number is divisable by 9).

Also, looking at the pattern of the multiples of 3, it is interesting to see. Within the first 10 (1-10), they are 3, 6, and 9. Within the next 10 (11-20), the multiples are 12, 15, 18, which shows that the ones columns are one less than in the first 10. Then, the next 10 (21-30), the multiples are 21, 24, and 27. Then, it lands on 30, which of course is 3 times 10. After that, it starts all over: 33, 36, 39, etc. This may seem trivial or unimportant, but learning this and then remembering this makes using the number 3 so much easier. If nothing else, it then makes logical sense, as all math does.

As I will show, it is also helpful to do the same thing with all of the other numbers, to see the pattern of the multiples. Also, this will make even more sense when you review all of the multiples using and visualizing with My Pattern or **Nelson's Train Stops**.

Four (4):

Four is 4 more than 0, but is 1 less than 5. It is 6 less than 10. Therefore, adding a 1 to a four is always 5; adding a 6 to 4 is always a 10. Subtracting a 4 from 10 is 6 and subtracting a 6 is 4. This same relationship exists with any number ending in 4 or 6

Since the 4 is one less than 5, the student can use a trick by adding a 4 to any number by adding a 5 and subtract a 1. So you can use the Rule of 5's and simply go backwards 1 number or spot.

For example: Add 4 to 23 (4 + 23): Use the Rule of 5s and add 5 which is 28, but then go back 1 which gives you the answer: 27. I will show how to do this more on my crossover technique.

Let's look at the multiples of 4. 4 is an even number and twice as much as a 2. Therefore, every other 2 is divisable by 4; that means ½ of all even numbers are multiples of 4. However, if it is divisable by 4, then it is always divisable by 2. This is just like the same relationship as 5 and 10.

All 10's are even numbers and always divisable by 2. However, since only ½ of even numbers are divisable by 4, then only ½ of all 10's are divisable by 4. Interesting is that if the 10's digit is an even number (and a 0 at the end), then it is divisable by a 4.

Within the first 10 numbers: the multiples of 4 are 4 and 8; within the second 10 the multiples are 12, 16, & 20 (2 is even number); within the third 10: 24, 28; and the fourth 10: 32, 36, and then 40. As you can see the pattern starts over after the 2nd 10, or in the 20's; or 4 times 5. Therefore, it will land on every other multiple of 10 and equivalent to 4 times any multiple of 5. This also shows that if a 5 is multiplied by an even number, it will land on a multiple of 10. Again, be sure to visualize on a pattern.

Six (6)

Six (6) is 6 more than 0, and is 1 more than 5. It is 4 less than 10. Therefore, subtracting a 1 from a 6 is always 5; adding a 4 to 6 is always a 10. Subtracting a 4 from 10 is 6 and subtracting a 6 is 4. This same relationship exists with any number ending in 4 or 6. Since 6 is one more than 5, the student can use a trick when adding a 6 to any number. Add a 5 then add a 1 more. So you can use the Rule of 5's and simply go forwards 1 number or spot.

For example: Add 6 to 39 (6 + 39). Use the Rule of 5s and add 5 going to 44, but then go forward 1 which gives you the answer: 45. This goes along with the fact that if you add a 6 to a number ending in 4, then you can go to the next 10; if add 6 to a 9, then go to the next 5.

Let's look at the multiples of 6. Six is an even number and twice as much as a 3. Therefore, the six is divisable by 3; so there might be some similarities. Just because a number ends in 3 or 6 doesn't mean it is divisable by 3 or 6. The multiples of 6 (six) include: 6, 12, 18, 24, 30, 36, 42, 48, 54, 60. As you can see, the multiples are all even numbers but the last digit is a 6 only once, until you reach 30. 30 is a multiple of 5 and 6. At that point, the pattern starts over with the next number ending in 6. (36). This also shows that if a 5 is multiplied by an even number, it will land on a multiple of 10.

Seven (7)

Seven (7) is 7 more than 0, and is 2 more than 5. It is 3 less than 10. Therefore, subtracting a 2 from a 7 is always 5; adding a 3 to 7 is always a 10. Subtracting a 3 from 10 is 7 and subtracting a 7 is 3. This same relationship exists with any number ending in 7. Since the 7 is two more than 5, the student can use a trick when adding a 7 to another number. One can add a 5 then add a 2. So you can use the Rule of 5's and simply go forwards 2 numbers or spot.

For example: Add 7 to 45 (7 + 45). Use the Rule of 5s and add 5 going to 50, but then go forward 2 which gives you the answer: **52.** Which goes along with the fact that if you add a 7 to a number ending in 3, then you can go to the next 10; if add 7 to an 8, then go to the next 5.

Let's look at the multiples of 7. 7 is an odd number and has no easy pattern. The multiples of 7 (seven) include: 7, 14, 21, 28, 35, 42, 49, 56, 63, and 70. As you can see, the multiples have little relation to each other. Every other multiple is an even number, as is the case anytime an odd number is multiplied with an even number it becomes an even number. It helps to know that 7 times 5 is 35, which ends in 5 and therefore, a multiple of 5.

We talked earlier about the patterns starting over again. For 7, it does not start over again until 7 times 10 which is 70.

Eight (8):

Eight (8) is 8 more than 0, and is 3 more than 5. It is 2 less than 10. Therefore, subtracting a 3 from an 8 is always 5; adding a 2 to 8 is always a 10. Subtracting a 2 from 10 is 8 and subtracting an 8 is 2. This same relationship exists with any number ending in 2 or 8. Since the 8 is 3 more than 5, the student can use a trick when adding an 8 to another number. One can add a 5 then add a 3; or add a 10 and subtract 2. So you can use the Rule of 5's and add a 3; or the Rule of 10's and subtract a 2.

For example: Add 8 to 53 (8 + 53). Use the Rule of 5s and add 5 going to 58, but then go forward 3 which gives you the answer; OR, add a 10 to 53 and subtract a 2: Answer: 61. One can also learn that adding a 3 to an 8, is always one more than 2 + 8; which is 10 + 1= 11. So 53 + 8 is intuitively 61. This goes along with the fact that if you add an 8 to a number ending in 2, then you can quickly go to the next 10.

Let's look at the multiples of 8. Eight is an even number and twice as much as a 4. Therefore, the 8 is divisable by 4; so there are some similarities. Just because a number ends in 4 or 8 doesn't mean it is divisible by 4 or 8. The multiples of 8 (eight) include: 8, 16, 24, 32, 40, 48, 56, 64, 72, 80. As you can see, the multiples are all even numbers but the last digit is an 8 only once, until you reach 40. 40 is a multiple of 5 and 8. At that point, you start over with the next number ending in 8. (48). This also shows that if a 5 is multiplied by an even number, it will land on a multiple of 10. All should be viewed on a visual pattern or **Nelson's Train Stops** Game.

Nine (9)

Nine (9) is 9 more than 0, is 4 more than 5 and 1 less than 10. Therefore, adding a 1 to a 9 is always 10; adding a 9 to 1 is always a 10. Subtracting a 9 from 10 is 1 and subtracting a 1 from 10 is 9. This same relationship exists with any number ending in 9 or 1. Since the 9 is one less than 10, the student can use a trick when adding a 9 to another number. One can add a 10 and subtract a 1. So you can use the Rule of 10's and simply go backwards 1 number or spot.

For example: Add 9 to 28 (9 + 28). Use the Rule of 10s and add 10 going to 38, but then go back 1 which gives you the answer: 37. You could also subtract 1 from 28 first, then add 10, which is the same: 37.

Another aspect of adding 9 is that anytime you add a 9, you are moving to the next 10's level, but then the last digit is one less. This is similar to the Rule of 10s, but then move back one. This may seem the same as the first technique, but it actually eliminates a step. Using the same example: adding 9 to 28 means that it automatically goes to the 30s level, and is one less than 8 = 37. However, having both techniques available in your memory gives you a back up and a check of your computation.

You can also use the crossover technique by using 2 of the nine to get to 30, then with the 7 left, add to 30 and you have 37. You could also use the rule of 5's by adding 5 to 28, which gives you 33; then you have 4 left, then add this which gives you 37. This again shows how different techniques can be used, and you will find which one works best for any particular situation.

Let's look at the multiples of 9. Nine is an odd number, so every other multiple is an even number. The multiple numbers are 9, 18, 27, 36, 45,

54, 63, 72, 81, 90, and 99. As you move up through the multiples, each of the "one's" digits gets smaller by one with each move up. You can see easily that you can add 10 then minus 1 each time.

An unusual rule with 9 is that like the 3, it is easy to determine if any number is a mulitple of 9 or can be divided by 9. Take any number and add the digits together. If they add up to 9 or a multiple of 9, then it is divisable by 9. As you can see the multiples, add the digits, and they all equal 9. All should be viewed and learned on a visual pattern or **Nelson's Train Stops** Game, as this will make all of these more logical and easily used.

We have now reviewed the basic rules for the numbers 1-10. The numbers over 10 have similar rules as those 1-10; however, I thought there would be some value to mention a few prinicples of some of these numbers. Remember that every number has its own rules and principles. The more you can learn them, the easier it will be to use the numbers for computations.

Eleven (11)

Eleven (11) is interesting in that it is simply two ones put together. Properties are similar to a one, but in both the tens and ones digit. Adding eleven to any number means you only need to add a one to both the 10s and 1s digit. For example, add 11 to 37. As above, you can use the rule of 10's by adding a 10, then adding a one. Therefore, you would: 37+10= 47, then 47+1= 48. Or you can add a one to the 3 (10s digit), then add a 1 to the 7 and come up with 48.

Subtracting eleven means you subtract a one from each column. If you are subtracting 2 numbers and the smaller number has one less in each column, the answer is 11.

Multiples of 11 can be seen by adding 11 to itself; which then are: 22, 33, 44, and so on. All of the numbers, up to 99, with the same number in the 10s and one's digit, is divisable by 11. Once it gets past 99, then the next multiple is 110. As you can see it is 11 x 10, which means you only have to add a zero (0) to the end of the eleven. It is also interesting to see 11 multiplied by 20, 30, 40, etc.

An example: I am watching Indianapolis Colts just beat the Denver Broncos, and they won 24-13. Well both columns subtract 1, so the difference in their score is 11. This is what makes numbers fun and relevent multiple times a day. What is the total score? Well, you can add both columns, or you can use the rule of 13 or three's. I would add a 10 (34) then add another 3 = 37. This also shows how you can use multiple opportunities to practice using numbers and math.

Twelve (12):

Twelve (12) is an important number, because 12 is used in many common measurements in daily life. There are 12 inches in each foot, and there are 12 items in dozen, and 12 hours on a clock. Therefore, computing multiples of 12 is important and a common occurrence. It has a one in the 10s and 2 in the ones digit. So you can add simply by adding the columns, or you can use the rule of 10s and add a 2. For example: 12 + 53: Use the Rule of 10's by adding 10 to the 53, then add another 2 = 65.

Multiples are 12, 24, 36, 48, 60, 72, 84, 96, 108, and 120. The first 4 multiples progress up only one in the 10s digit, however, at 60 it skips a 10 and goes to 60. This is also 12 times 5. Again, an even number times 5 will end up being a multiple of 10, or have a 0 at the end. This then progresses up 1 in the 10s again up until 120 or 12 x 10.

Fifteen (15):

Fifteen (15) ends in a five, therefore, it is a multiple of 5; but then also 3. So 3 x 5 = 15. You can utilize the multiples; however, the use of 15 occurs frequently. Learning to add and subtract 15 may be useful. You can add a five to the ones column and a 1 to the tens. You can add in steps: add 10 first then a 5 or the other way around. When subtracting, you can subtract a 10 then a 5, or the other way around.

Multiples of 15 are 15, 30, 45, 60, 75, 90, 105, 120, 135, and 150. It is interesting that 60 and 120 are common to 12. It helps to know that 15 goes into each one, and what the other multiplier is. Knowing that 15 x 2 is 30 makes it is easy to compute 60 / 4 (= 15), and 90 / 6 (=15).

Sixteen (16)

Sixteen (16) also is a common number. There are 16 ounces in a pint, and then 32 ounces in a quart. So it frequently comes up in measurements. It has several numbers that it is divisable by: 2, 4, 8. Its multiples are 16,

32, 48, 64, 80, 96, and 112. Interesting is that 80 is the product of 16 x 5; which is halfway to 160 (10x16).

Eighteen (18)

Eighteen (18) is another common number. It is a multiple of 2 (even number), 3, 6, & 9. As you can see, the 1+8 (of 18) is 9, so that tells you it is divisable by 9. Its multiples are also worth remembering: 18, 36, 54, 72, and 90. Notice that 5 times 18 is 90, a multiple of 10.

Twenty (20) & other "TENS" (Multiples of 10: 20, 30, 40, 50, 60, 70, 80, 90, 100)

Twenty is another common number but is a multiple of 10. I already reviewed the number "0", but I am lumping the multiples of 10 together here. They use similar principles and rules as a 10 and their associated digit.

When you add "a 10" (multiples of 10), you can look at them in a couple different ways. When you add anything to one of these, then you can use the Rule of 10s from before. For example: 30 + 8 is easily computed to 38 because the 8 is added on to a "10". Or you can use the same Rule of 10s and you end up with the same last digit, but then you jump 3 "10s". Or then you can simply add the number in the 10s digit to the other number.

For example: 30 + 27. You know that the answer will have a 7 in the final digit. Then use the Rule of 10's but you have to jump 3 tens to get there: 37, 47, and then 57. You can also simply add the 10's digits (2+3= 5), then add the one's digits (0+7 = 7); therefore = 57.

If subtracting, you simply do the opposite, but use the same rules. For example: 40 – 7, you would use the Rule of 10s by simply knowing the prinicple of 7s and that it is 3 short of 10, and easily come up with 33. If the example is: 67-40, then you know that the answer will have a 7 in the final digit, and you would have to jump down 4 "10s", thus giving you the answer; Or, simply subtract 4 from 6 and leave the 7 alone. (= 27).

I believe it is important to learn all three methods, because this then will allow the child to "understand" the principles better.

In multiplying and dividing, you can use the Rule of 10s, however, there is a different number in the "tens" column. So whatever you do, then you have to multiply the tens by that number. But, more than likely, it is probably easier to simply use the principles of each corresponding number, but you multiply and divide and then place or remove a zero at the end. For example: 20 x 18: You might think that you could take 2 times 1 and have your answer, however, you must multiply the entire number by 2, then add a zero. (=360).

Take another example: 99/ 30: You have to divide by the entire number, then take away a 0. In this case 99/3 = 33; so in order to take away a zero, you have to move the decimal place to the left one space; with the answer being 3.3. However, this is probably outside the scope of this book, but essential to understand at some point.

Twenty-five (25):

Twenty-five (25) is a common number. Probably the most common use is the "quarter" (coin) which is 25 cents. Since it is called a "quarter", it designates ¼ th (a quarter) of a dollar (100 cents). This means that there are 4 quarters in a dollar. Some pretty basic information, but you should make sure children understand this principle before moving on. Correlating money with numbers such as this is another great tool for children to understand numbers and money and how they are connected. Therefore, using penneys, nickels, dimes, quarters, and all money are highly recommended, and gives another visual for the child to understand. You could also begin to teach interest rates, stocks, and bonds; or maybe wait a year or two.

Fifty (50):

Fifty (50) is another common number. It is one-half (1/2) of 100, 2 quarters or (2x25). It is an even number, a multiple of 5, and a multiple of 10. There is also a 50 cent piece coin. I often think of 50 as the halfway point to 100. And it the halfway point on my game: ***Nelson's Train Stops.*** Since it has a 5 in the 10's column, it has similar properties as a 5 and a 10. A child could learn to count by 50s to go up to 1000.

Seventy-five (75):

Seventy-five (75) is a multiple of 25 and is three-fourths (3/4) of 100. This would represent 3 quarters. Seventy five is also interesting with its multiples: 150, 225, 300, 375, 450, 525, and 600.

One Hundred (100):

One Hundred (100) is very common and has many common traits with other numbers. It is an even number; is a multiple of 5 and 10, so therefore has similar rules as 5 and 10. It is 10 x 10; or 5 x20; or 25x4; or 50x2. It also begins the transition to the "100s. It then sets up the rules for 100, which all of the "hundreds" use. For a pattern or grid, getting to 100 starts a transition to the hundreds grid. This you can see in **Figure 2**. The 100 then repeats itself up to 100 (Figure 2). Then it repeats itself again all the way up to 1000. For a game such as ***Nelson's Train Stops***, it is at the end of this game, but could still go up from there.

Multiples of 100:

Multiples of 100: (200, 300, 400, 500, 600, 700, 800, 900) all have similar properties as 100, but with different numbers in hundred's spot. They also have similar properties as each individual number (2, 3, 4, ...)

When adding or subtracting one of the hundreds, use the similar property as 100, but with a larger number in the hundreds spot. For example, 27+300 is easy in that 27 can be added onto the base 300, and equals 327. Even though this seems simple, it uses the same rule as 27 added to 0 or 100. For 400 + 179, you would add 4 to the 1 spot (hundred's column) and come up with 579.

For multiplying and dividing, you would use the same type of principle as the "10s" above. However, in this case, you add 2 zeros at the end (multiplication). As before, you have to multiply the entire number by the hundred's number. For example: 37 x 200; use the 2 in two hundred to multiply 37 x 2 which is 74 and add on the 2 zero's to become 7400.

For division, you again divide the entire number by the hundred's number, then take away 2 zero's or move 2 decimal points. For example: divide 8800 by 400: means you take 8800 and divide by 4 which is 2200, then take away 2 zeros which equals 22. There are also other methods to use with division, and probably outside the scope here. However, I wanted to show this for completeness.

Above 100:

As above, I have a system to visualize all of the numbers, even those over 100. Going up to 1000, I repeat each set of 100. So the pattern from

100 to 200 looks the same as 1-100, however, one "level" up. I then go up to the 200s, the 300s, and so forth up to 1000. **Figure 2** demonstrates how the pattern/ map works and looks like. As you go higher, the details of the pattern look smaller and smaller, while including more and more numbers into the pattern.

Some common numbers are 125 & 250 & 500. All are mutiples of 25. 250 and 500 are multiples of 50.

One hundred-twenty five (125) is 1/8th of 1000 and comes up frequently, and is 25 x 5. Multiples are 125, 250, 375, 500, 625, 750, 875, and 1000. These would also correlate with multiples of 12.5 and relationship with 100; however, as you can see, 12.5 is 1/10th of 125.

Two hundred-fifty (250) is ¼ of 1000 (or 4 x 250 = 1000) and can be used as a reference point when doing math in this area. This is similar to 25 and relationship with 100.

Five hundred (500) is ½ of 1000 and again a common reference point.

These are all good visual reference points. Seeing where these numbers are on a pattern helps give a reference for the rest of the numbers.

One Thousand (1000):

One thousand (1000) is a significant milestone in numbers. It is a common reference point, and a turning point in My Pattern/Grid. My first part of the My Pattern is to 100, but then it repeats up to 1000. At 1000, then the entire pattern starts all over. I explained it above in Chapter 3, however, will rehash here.

After 1000 and moving to 1001, you begin the second 1000. You then duplicate everything you have done and seen in the first 1-1000, however, you put a 1 in front (or 1 in the thousand's column). Then use the same pattern all the way up to 2000.

Also, the transition at 1000 begins a different level in My Pattern". From here, each 1000 has its own space or box, and looks like the original 1-10, then 1-100, then 1-1000 as what we started with. However, within each space, there are 1000 numbers squeezed into each space.

To state a different way, I start over with the same 1-100 pattern that then goes up to 1000. I then put 1000 numbers into this next level pattern.

This means that each 1 is equivalent to 1000. Therefore, an 8000 would look like the number 8 on the original Grid.

The rules and principles of 1000 are very similar to 1, 10, and 100; however, it has another zero at the end.

Anything added to 1000, would simply be the same as adding to a zero, but then place a one in the "thousands" column. For example: 1000 + 375=1375. If the other number is greater than 1000, then you use the similar principles as 100. Simply add a one in the thousand's column. To subtract, simply take a one from the thousand's column.

Multiplication and division is similar to 1, 10, and 100, however, 1000 has 3 zeros. So take the number times 1 and add three zero's; or simply add on 3 zeros. To divide, you would take away 3 zero's. Examples include: 83 x 1000 = 83000; 357 x 1000 = 357,000; 5000 / 1000 = 5; 123,000/ 1000= 123.

Above 1000 and beyond:

As described above, going over 1000 starts a new level of "My Pattern", but it is also similar to a 100 with another zero at the end. As above, it is always good to understand what happens when adding a zero. From 1000, the pattern then totally repeats itself.

In other words, each one thousand is the equivalent of one on the original pattern. So, when I see 5 thousand, I actually looks like the original "5" on the 1-100 map, however, it contains an entire 1000 within each of the 1-5 numbers or spaces.

So 1000 to 100,000 will look like the original 1-100 Pattern, but then repeats itself all the way up to 1000; and since each space has 1000 numbers, it is equivalent to 1,000,000 (1 million). Each of the 1000 numbers or spaces contain 1000 numbers or spaces within.

Any type of mathematics (adding, subtracting, multiplying, and division) at this level is difficult to do in your head, so each column is laid out and performed in the usual school taught fashion. However, when performing these, this gives you a much better perspective of what you are accomplishing, and what it looks like. My correlations are above.

One Million (1,000,000)

One million (1,000,000) is a milestone in many ways. Everyone dreams of having a million dollars. The term one million seems enormous, and anytime a million of anything is shown, it appears incredibly high. Have you ever started counting to 1 million? 1 million seconds = 278 hours; or 11 ½ days.

One million is the next major milestone in "My Pattern", which starts "My Pattern" over again. Every time you add on 3 zeros, or every multiple of 1000, starts the pattern over again. Counting by 1, 2, 3, ... million will look like the original 1-100 pattern again. Every number or space is equivalent to 1,000,000 numbers or spaces contained within, which contains the entire 1 – 1 million pattern. This is further explained well above.

The principles of 1,000,000 then are similar to all of the other numbers with a 1 plus zeros: 10, 100, 1000, 10,000, 100,000. Also, it is important to remember that 1000 x 1000 = 1 million. Therefore, 1 million is 1000 thousands. That is why there are 1000 numbers within each 1 thousand space, up to 1000 spaces, which then is 1 million.

In addition and subtraction, when you add 1,000,000, it is similar to adding to zero, but then add the necessary zeros and a one in the "millions' column.

Multiplying and dividing is the same as the other numbers with a 1 and zeros behind. Take the number times 1 and place the zeros to the right. For example: 943 x 1,000,000 = 943,000,000. Or you can simply place the zeros on the number. Dividing means taking away 6 zeros or moving decimal to left 6 spaces.

Moving up the millions, the pattern continues to look like the original 1-1000, but with 1 million numbers in each one. Any type of mathematics (adding, subtracting, multiplying, and division) at this level is difficult to do in your head, so each column is laid out and performed in the usual school taught fashion. However, when performing these, this gives you a much better perspective of what you are accomplishing, and what it looks like. My correlations are above.

One Billion (1,000,000,000):

One billion (1,000,000,000) is 1000 times 1 million, or you can place 3 more zeros at the end. On the way up to one billion, you put 1 million numbers or pieces into every box up to 1000. So it is 1000 millions.

Every time you add 3 zeros, "My Pattern" starts all over again. So looking at the original 1-100 grids, imagine there are 1 billion numbers in each spot, which then goes up to 100 billion. After that, the 100 billion repeats itself up to 1000 billion, which then becomes One Trillion (1,000,000,000,000). Then I start over again.

The properties are similar with this number as all the numbers that have 1 with zero's behind it. It is a multiple of 5, 10, 100, 1000, and 1,000,000. You can add a number to 1 billion and then have one billion plus the number or add 1 to the billion's column.

One Trillion (1,000,000,000,000) and Beyond:

Once you reach One Trillion, you feel you have reached a very large number. However, in fact our national debt is now $16.7 Trillion Dollars. ($16,787,451,118,147) (at the time of writing this). Imagine now that in order to get to this, you have go up to 16 on my original pattern, with 1 trillion dollars in each space or box. The budget proposed by President Obama currently (February 2015) is a projected $4 Trillion dollars. After reading this book, you now realize how large this number is.

Properties for One Trillion continue to be the same as the other multiples of 1000, 1,000,000, and 1,000,000,000.

As numbers grow towards infinity, there continues to be an entire set of increasing larger numbers. Every time the numbers repeat themselves a thousand times (or adding 000), then the number gets renamed. This also means that every time there is a new name, "My Pattern" starts all over again. So when you have gone through "My Pattern" up to 1000 Trillion, you then come to: Quadrillion. After that, it is Quintillion, Sextillion, and then even more. (See **Addendum D**).

In fact, you probably don't know that there is a very large number called: "Googol". It is 10 to the 100th power, or a 1 with a hundred zero's behind it. The term was coined in 1938 by 9-year-old Milton Sirotta, nephew of American mathematician Edward Kasner. Kasner popularised the concept in his 1940 book *Mathematics and the Imagination.* (Wikipedia, accessed on 2/12/15).

Infinity:

Infinity – If you didn't know already, numbers go into infinity, which means they never end. My Grid can essentially go on towards infinity, even though once you get passed trillions, it probably loses its effectiveness. The fact that numbers never end, and go to "Infinity", makes the term and concept very interesting with much written about it.

Negative Numbers:

Up until now, I have talked only about positive numbers, and I won't spend a lot of time with negative numbers here. However, I do see the entire spectrum of negative numbers, just like positive numbers, only in reverse. Even though, I don't have the need for using my pattern in reverse very often. However, my very brief summary is that my negative numbers use the same pattern but simply a mirror image.

Looking at the 1-100 pattern, imagine being asked to subtract a larger number from a smaller number. This would cause you to go below 0, which then goes into the negative numbers (-1, -2, -3,…) and use the pattern in reverse by using a mirror image of my pattern. You would use the same principles and rules, but in reverse.

Fractions:

Fractions are a little more complicated, but I do have a visual for fractions. Simple fractions alone fall between the space between 0 and 1. So, I need to use a separate grid to visualize fractions in that space. I use a type of drop down grid to visualize these fractions and would run from smaller to larger: 1/16, 1/8, ¼, ½, 5/8, ¾, 7/8, and any other fraction that might occur between 0-1.

Summary:

That should be enough numbers rules for now. This gives you a good start, because I would not consider this a complete list. I would be interested in hearing from teachers who could add to this list. This may seem like a lot, however there are hundreds of other rules that are not included. Remember that every number has its own rules and principles.

I don't know if all of these rules are being actively taught in schools today. However, it seems that some students are not getting the concepts or putting it all together. Therefore, I hope this type of explanation along with visualizing each rule on "My Pattern" will at least help with learning the concepts. It's also possible that teachers might use my principles and then add to those. It's possible that students may have trouble with certain concepts and the teacher may then refer to my methods. I also believe that if you learn several rules for the same numbers and math, it will greatly help your understanding of everything. It also shows that the more you look at a pattern and play with the numbers, you can come up with your own rules and the best way for you to remember how each computation can be done.

The goal is to "know" and "see" each rule, as you work with numbers; not to memorize and rely on this memory when doing problems. Therefore, it is imperative to learn and use these principles with some type of "visual" of "My Pattern" or a game such as ***Nelson's Train Stops.***

CHAPTER 5

Rules and Principles of Math

You now know many of the rules and principles of numbers that I believe are extremely helpful and I have used throughout my life. You can build upon that by learning these rules and adding your own. This is not a comprehensive list, but the more you learn the better. Even though math teachers teach numbers and math rules, this may be a unique perspective for them or you. The goal is to use what works best for you or the child and to put them all together and use on a daily basis.

The last chapter was a little long because I wanted to cover most of the rules and principles that have used myself and feel important. This chapter will not be quite as long and cumbersome as I just need to use the principles already learned to put to use in math computations.

The Rules of Math may seem to be the same as or very similar to the Rules and Principles of Numbers. There is a lot of overlap; however, it's important to know the rules of numbers before getting to the rules of math.

As you or the child performs math problems, there will be times, when going back to review the principles of the numbers themselves will be helpful. Knowing the rules of each number individually will then make math much easier.

One of the benefits of using a visual in math, is that it gives you a perspective of the numbers, as I discussed above. However, another advantage or tool is that it can also give you a type of a map. When you look at a map, you will look at it in perspective to where you currently are, where you have to go, and how to get there. When you get directions on how to go somewhere, this is in relationship to where you are starting. Therefore, using a visual for math allows you to see where you are starting and then when given the directions (math problem), you can then see the final answer, or your destination. That is what a game such as **Nelson's Train Stops** will do for you and your child/ student. I will present my principles below in more of a conventional way, but then make reference to how to use the visual with a starting point. It is usually easier to use the larger number as the reference point, however, if playing a game, that may not be possible. Therefore, it is important to learn both ways. If you get directions to travel somewhere, you will need to know how to get back.

Finally, the goal of learning the principles of numbers and math is to perform while using a visual, then continual repetition. The student/ child should get good enough to be able to know the answers to as many math problems and formula's without thinking. I personally look at many problems and don't see the problem, only the answer.

Addition:

Adding is just an advanced form of counting, but on an advanced stage. It is a way to count smaller numbers on up to larger numbers without doing the actually counting. The child may start by counting forward, or "steps", as in a game. Next, he/she needs to refer to the rules of each number outlined above. As the numbers and moves get bigger, then the child will begin learning some of the principles of math.

One (1): Adding 1 is just like counting; just the next number, or step forward. However, the child needs to be able know this automatically. This seems intuitive, but not necessarily to a young child. For example adding a 1 to 7, should allow the child to respond quickly to the answer (8). Use the other number as the reference point, then adding the one will be simple and easy to see.

Two (2): Adding 2 is similar to counting 2, and a good start for any child. However, then go to the rules for "2". For example, adding a 2 to an even number is then the next even number. If 2 is added to an odd number, then you go to the next odd number.

Using the other number as a reference, you can see where you ae starting and where you are in relation to a 5 or 10. If on a 3, then you already know you are 2 away from 5. If on an 8, then you know you are 2 away from 10. If on a 5 or 10, then you use the rules of 5 and 10 as you know 7 is 2 more than 5, and 12 is 2 more than 10. If on a nine, then you can use the cross-over technique: use 1 to get to 10, then use the other 1 to get to 11. If you are on 7 or 6, then you know you are 3 or 4 spaces away from 10, which then gives you the answers: 9 and 8.

Three (3): Adding 3 can be started by counting as above, then use the rules of 3. Know that three is 2 less than a 5 and 7 less than 10. Therefore, you can see how far you are from the next 5 (or 10). If you are closer than 3, then you will use the crossover technique. Adding a 3 to 2 (3 + 2), then you should know automatically that the answer is 5. Adding a 3 to 3 (3+3), then it is simply a doubling of 3, to 6. 3 + 4: then use the cross-over technique by using 1 to get to 5 and then add the remaining 2 which equals 7.

Use the other number as a reference or starting point. If on 6, then 3 is a multiple of 6 and so just add on another 3 to 9. If on 7, then you know 7 is 3 less than 10, and therefore = 10. If on 8 or 9, then use the crossover technique for 10, use 2 or 1 and then add the remaining; equaling 11 and 12. If on 10, then it's just like adding to zero: = 13.

Four (4): Adding 4 can also be started by counting. Four is 1 less than 5. Therefore, you can use the same principle as "5s", then subtract 1; or you can subtract a one first, then add a 5; Or just know that 4 is one less than 5. Again, know where you are starting from, and use the same type of principles I outlined with the above 1-3. If on "1", then adding 4 is simply 5, as 4 is one less than 5. Four is also 6 less than 10, so know that 4+6=10. Four plus 2 would use the same principle as the 2's (next even number), or, use the Rule of 5s and add a 1 to 5, then another 1 to 6. Adding 4 to 3 can use the crossover at 5, (Add 2 to 3 = 5, then 2 more = 7). 7+4 will use knowledge that 7 is 3 less than 10, then 1 is left over. 8+4 also uses the crossover, with knowledge of 8+2=10, then add 2 more. Also, 4 is a multiple of 8 and therefore, just add another 4, which is 4x3=12.

If you are not given a "starting point" such as you would if you are playing a game, but only given a problem, which number do use as the starting point? (For example with 4 + 3) It is usually easier to use the larger number as the reference or starting point, however, it is important to know both. Do the easier method first, but then check yourself by using the other way. Adding 3 to 4 -> Add 1 to 4=5, plus 2 more = 7; Adding 4 to 3 = Add 2 to 3=5, then 2 more = 7.

Five (5): Adding Five (5) should be relatively simple as you use the Rule of the 5s. Also, use the prinicples of the number being added to, as all numbers have a relationship with 5s. See how adding 5 puts the answer in the same relationship as it was before. In other words the answer should be equal distance from the 5 where you started and the next 5. For example: Add 5 to 8 (5 + 8). 8 is 2 less than 10 and 3 more than 5. Moving up to the next 5: 13 is 2 less than 15 and 3 more than 10, therefore, = 13. This can be easily seen on a grid or pattern, and learned. To perform the same problem (5+8), you can also use the crossover technique: (Add 2 to 8=10, then add the remaining 3 to 10=13).

Ten (10): Adding Ten (10) should also be relatively simple as you use the Rule of 10s. We spent lots of time on 10 and the "10s" back in Chapter 3. Therefore, start with the principles you already have learned. Adding a 10, you can simply add a 1 to the "10s column", or go to the next number with the same last digit, but at the next 10 level. It is also similar to adding the number to zero, but then putting a "1" in the 10s digit. Therefore, you could use either 10 or the other number as a reference or starting point. For example: 10 + 7: Using the 7 as the reference point, then you could either move up to the next "10 level" from 7 to give you a 17; or, simply place a one in front of the 7 = 17. If 7 + 10, and use 10 as the reference point, then adding 7 to 10 is similar to adding to 0, but at the next 10 level or add a one to the 10s digit = 17.

Tens: With a multiple of 10 (eg, 20, 30, …) you can use the same principles as the 10, except, you have a different number in the 10s digit. You again can use either number as the reference point, but certainly easier to use the "10 multiple" as the reference. For example: 9 + 30 (adding 9 to 30, using 30 as the reference), think of adding 9 to a zero, but only starting with 30, = 39. If you add 30 to 9 (30 + 9), then you would jump to the next 10 level three times, or simply add a 3 to the 10s digit in front of the 9 = 39. You could also think of the principles of "9", which you could add 10 to 30, then subtract a 1 = 39.

You might find the difference in all of these methods cumbersome and not worth the effort to learn. As I discussed above, learning as many methods and principles of numbers and math as possible adds to your perspective and understanding. You will find which one might work for you. You also may use different methods for different situations or problems.

Adding numbers 6-9 utilize similar principles as those already presented above. You would use the rules and principles of each as presented in Chapter 4. However, each is related to a corresponding number from 1 – 4, as they are separated by 5. For example: Six is 1+5, Seven: 2+5, Eight: 3+5; Nine: 4+5. Therefore, you can use the crossover technique, add the amount to get to 5 or 10, then add on the remaining amount. Since they are closer to 10, then you can use crossover technique for all when crossing 10.

Six (6) is 1 more than 5 and it is 4 less than 10. When adding a six (6) on to any number, you can use the Rule of 5s, then add one more. When adding another number onto 6, then you can add 4 up to 10, then add on the remaining amount (crossover technique). Example include: Add 6 to 7: you can add a 5 to 7 =12, then 1 more = 13 (Rule of 5s). Add 8 to 6: first add 4 to 6, then 4 more to equal 14 (crossover technique).

Seven (7) is 2 more than 5 and is 3 less than 10. When adding a seven (7) onto a reference number, you can use the Rule of 5s, then add 2 more. When adding another number onto 7, then you can add 3 up to 10, then add on the remaining amount. Some examples: Add 7 onto 8: you can add a 5 to = 13, then 2 more = 15 (Rule of 5s). Add 9 to 7: first add 3 to the 7 to = 10, then add 6 more = 16. (Crossover technique). However, this same problem, since using a nine (9), you can use the rule of 10s by: add a 10 to 7 (=17) then minus a 1 = 16.

Eight (8) is 3 more than 5 and 2 less than 10. When adding an eight (8) onto a reference number, you can use the Rule of 5s, then add 3 more. When adding another number onto 8, then you can add 2 up to 10, then add on the remainng amount. For examples: Add 8 onto 6: you can add 5 to 6 (=11), then add 3 more = 14 (Rule of 5s). Add 4 onto 8: first add 2 (=10) then add 2 more = 12 (Cross over technique). You can also use 8 to add 10 and subtract 2 (Rule of 10s).

Nine (9) is 4 more than 5 and is 1 less than 10. Therefore, you can use the rule of 5s plus 4, or #4 then 5. Even better, you can add 10 and subtract 1 (Rule of 10s). Or just remember that 9 is one less than 10 and make quick adjustment. When adding another number to 9, you can use 1 of the number, then add on the remaining portion (crossover technique).

All of the rest of the numbers use the principles outlined above in Chapter 4. There are many other rules and principles you can use and for the child can learn. The earlier they learn the better. Again, be sure to use a visual pattern, such as **Nelson's Train Stops** Game, while you are reviewing all of the above. Children will learn in school, and can use, the traditional method of adding by lining up the problem and memorizing numbers and equations. However, I believe learning these principles greatly improve their perspective and understanding.

Finally, the goal is to learn the principles of numbers and math while using a visual, and repetition. This allows the student or child to become proficient enough to be able to perform computations with very little thought. The answers for many problems can be automatic. I often look at many problems and don't see problems, only the answer.

Subtracting:

Subtraction is similar to all of the principles of adding, however, it is in reverse. Subtraction can be described as counting backwards, and is a start. Any number subtracting a 1 is the same as counting backwards. Any other number subtracted requires more than just counting back one. That is why we learn subtracting. However, most of the time, it appears that learning subtraction is trying to memorize subtraction tables. The student needs to learn the principles of subtraction and visualize what it looks like at the same time. The goal is to know what subtraction equations are and what they look like, without having to rely on memorization.

The first rule of subtracting is that if you subtract a number from itself, the answer is always 0. In other words, whatever progress you made with the number is taken totally away by the subtraction. The second rule is that subtracting 0 from any number is the same number. You are not taking anything away from that number. The third rule is that the number subtracted and the answer are interchangeable. You always start with a reference number, and then you subtract a portion of the number to give the remaining amount. If you then switch those (last 2) numbers, then the formula remains accurate. For example: start with 14 as a reference point; subtract 8, which gives 6 as the answer ($14 - 8 = 6$). Then subtracting 6 from 14 then gives you 8. ($14 - 6 = 8$). This works this way every time. You don't need to know the names of each number, however for completeness: the first value is the *minuend*. The second value (the one you are subtracting) is called the *subtrahend*. The answer in a subtraction problem is called the *difference*.

One aspect of subtracting is that if the the number you start with (minuend) is less than the number you are subtracting (subtrahend), then the answer (difference) will be a negative number. So, all of my examples show the first number (start number) to be larger than the second (subtracting). This is the usual way of learning, and you are assuming you are starting with a specified amount of something, then taking away a portion of that total amount to see what would be left. I will discuss negative numbers briefly later.

Subtracting a one (1) is the same as counting backwards. The next step is to actually know and remember what is one less than any number. Again, you do this by visualizing exactly what you are doing. For example: 3-1, 5-1, 6-1, 10-1. The student/child should get good enough to be able to know the answers to these and all simple subtraction formula's without thinking. I personally look at these and don't see a problem, only the answer.

Subtracting a two (2) can be started by counting backwards two numbers or spaces, however you will want to progress from there. Subtracting 2 is similar to adding a two in that if the start number is even, then the anwer is the next even number in reverse. Subtracting a 2 from an odd number is then the next odd number in reverse. You will need to start with at least a 2, in order for the answer to be at least 0, and not a negative number. Start with the simplest computations: 3-2, 4-2, 5-2, then move up. It's helpful also to use the 5's and 10's as reference points. 5-2 =3 & 7-2=5. This shows both sides of 5 by 2; and the next shows both sides of 10: 10-2=8 & 12-2=10.

Also, part of subtraction is to know both numbers and the reverse additions. For example, 10-2 = 8; but then 10−8 = 2 and then 2+8 = 10. So, for every subtraction, there are two more associated problems that should be learned. Knowing all three and visualizing on a pattern, then increases your knowledge, understanding, perspective, and memory.

Subtracting a three (3) can also start with counting backwards, but again, progress from there. You need to start with at least a 3 in order to stay out of negative numbers. 4-3 should be easy (=1) but then use 5 and 10 as reference points: 5-3=2; 8-5=3; 10-3=7; 13-10=3. This uses all of the number's relationships with 5 and 10. You should know that 2 is 3 less than 5, 8 is 3 more than 5; 7 is 3 less than 10; and 13 is 3 more than 10. Three can also be thought of as 2+1, so subtracting a 1 then 2, or a 2 then 1 might be very helpful at times. For example: 7-3 can use 7-2 =5, then 5-1 =4; 6-3 can use 6-1 =5, then 5-2 =3. This is the crossover technique for subtraction.

Subtracting four (4) has several principles, as noted above. You can subtract in sections (2+2); or (3+1). You can also go backwards #2 even numbers, or #2 odd numbers. It is 1 less than 5 and then can use the Rule of 5 and then add 1. All of these are easily seen, used, and remembered if used with a visual pattern.

Subtracting five (5) uses the same Rule of 5s that you learned above. It uses the same principles as addition, but in reverse. All numbers (starting with 1-9) have a relationship with 5, so you can use those to solve problems. You can use the Rule of 5s on both sides of the subtraction formula. For example: 8-5=3; or 8-3=5. By knowing 8 is 3 more than 5, both of these problems are easily done. Also: 5-3=2; or 5-2=3; shows that knowing the relationships of 2 and 3 can be used. Remember that subtracting a 5 from a number ending with 5 will be a 10 or zero. Subtracting a 5 from "a 10", will give you a number ending in 5. For examples: 35-5 =30; and 40-5=35.

Subtracting ten (10) should also be relatively simple as you use the Rule of 10s. We spent lots of time on 10s back in Chapter 3. Therefore start with the principles you already have learned. If subtracting a 10, you can simply subtract a 1 to the "10s column", or go back to the next number with the same last digit, but at the 10 level before. With a multiple of 10 (eg, 20, 30,) you simply subtract the number to the 10s column; or go to the number with the same last digit, but go backwards the appropriate number of 10s. For example 24-20, you can subtract 2-2 and no change to 4, which equals 4; Or realize that you don't change the 4, but go back #2 – 10s and therefore = 4.

Subtracting numbers 6-9 are similar to their addition. I discussed this above as they are also similar to the corresponding numbers: 1-4. Think of each after subtracting 5: 6 – 5=1, 7 – 5= 2; 8 – 5 = 3, 9 – 5 = 4; which therefore uses the Rule of 5s. Be sure to remember to use the crossover technique for all when necessary. After some practice, the child should visualize and move to the appropriate spot based on the number itself.

Subtracting Six (6) can be seen as subtracting 1 then 5; or subtract 5 then 1, which uses the Rule of 5s minus 1 more. You can also use the crossover technique by subtracting 2 then 4; or subtract 3 then 3 more.

Subtracting Seven (7) can be seen as subtracting 2 then 5; or subtract 5 then 2, which uses the Rule of 5s minus 2 more. You can also use the crossover technique by subtracting 3 then 4; 1 then 6, or 2 then 5.

. Subtracting Eight (8) can be seen as subtracting 3 then 5; or subtract 5 then 3, which uses the Rule of 5s minus 3 more. You can also use the crossover technique by subtracting 4 then 4; or subtract 2 then 6 more.

Subtracting Nine (9) can be seen as subtracting 4 then 5; or subtract 5 then 4, which uses the Rule of 5s minus 4 more. You can also use the crossover technique by subtracting 2 then 7; or subtract 3 then 6 more. Or even better, you can subtract 10 (Rule of 10s) then add a 1. Or just remember that 9 is one less than 10 and make computation very quickly. (Eg, 25 – 9 ->; 25-5=20, then 4 more = 16; or: 25-10=15, but then add back 1; = 16.

For these numbers and any other number, be sure to review the rules of numbers as noted in the prior chapter. Every number has its own rules and principles, and by studying the principles, you will likely come up with your own techniques for addition and subtraction.

Cross Over Technique:

I already mentioned the crossover technique above, but will discuss further here. I bring it up here, as it can be used for both addition and subtraction. This is an example of a type of technique you can learn as part of learning "skills" in performing math. Some would call it "tricks", but I think of them as skills, and understanding of math principles. I don't know if this technique is being taught and/or learned, and I don't know if there may be another name for this, but is what I call it.

It is a technique used in both addition and subtraction. This is used whenever your addition or subtraction crosses a multiple of 5 or 10. Ideally, it could be used for crossing other numbers, such as 100 or 1000, and possibly even with multiplication or division. However, is outside my scope for here. There are a few different ways you can use the crossover technique.

One method is to add in sections. You actually split one of the numbers into 2 sections. The first portion gets you to the easiest reference point, usually the 5 or 10. Then use the portion that is left to finish the problem. Some examples:

- Eg, 3+4: Split the 3 into 2 parts: 1 & 2. Add the 1 to 4 to make 5, then add the remaining 2; which is 7. Also, you should automaticlly know that 7 is 2 more than 5 which makes the formula even easier.
- Eg, 7+8; Add 2 to 8, which takes you to 10, then you have 5 left, and then 10+5=15.
- Eg, 8+11; easily add 4 (=15), then add the remaining 4 (=19).

The crossover technique is similar to, but different than, using the Rule of 5s and the Rule of 10s. It also crosses over a 5 or 10, but uses the rules of 5 and 10 to find the answer. Find the number you start with and know the its relationship with the number being added (5 or 10). You then simply jump to the next 5 or 10 section.

- Eg, Add 5 to 8 (5 + 8). This shows that the answer (13) has the same relationship with a "5" as the eight does. 8 is 3 more than 5, and 13 is three more than 10, which is a multiple of 5. As you can see, you are jumping a "five", and get to the answer quickly.
- Eg, Add 10 to 8 (10+8). This is simple because you can just put a 1 in front of the 8. However, you can see that you are jumping from the section of 1-10, to 11-20, and keeping the same relationship. 8 is 8 more than 0, and 18 is 8 more than 10.
- Eg, Add 15 to 8 (15 + 8). This is similar but you would want to add the 5 to 8 first, which means you jump 5, but you can see that the answer 13 has the same relationship with a multiple of 5. Then jump another 10, and keep the same perspective. (Start with 13 and end with 23).

Using the cross over technique with Subtracting uses the same principles as using addition, but of course in reverse. Always know the principles of each number and how far they are from a 5 or 10. If you subtract 4 from 8 means that you "cross over" at 5. Split the 4 into 1 & 3, then subtract the 3 to bring to 5, and then subtract 1 more and equals 4. Other examples are:

- Eg, 9- 6: Subtract 4 from 9 which brings you to 5, then use the 2 left of the 6 to subtract down to 3. Another perspective you may have noticed is that 9 and 6 are both multiples of 3, so you are starting with #3 – 3s, then subtracting #2 – 3s and leaving =3.
- Eg, 13 – 7: Subtract 3 from thirteen to give you 10, then subtract the remaining 4 (of 7) from 10, and then = 6.
- Eg, 16 – 8: Here I would subtract a six from 16 to give you 10; then subtract the remaining 2 (of 8), and then = 8. You could also use the rule of eights; subtract a 10, then add back in a 2 = 8. Also, 8 is one-half of 16, which should be learned and remembered.
- Eg, 23- 7: Subtract 3 from 23 which =20, then use the remaining 4 (of 7) to subtract from 20 and give =16.

Always see where you are on the Pattern, and automatically you should see how far you are from the next 5 and 10. This means the 5 and 10 ahead and behind your current location. Remember, how many squares or spaces there are until the next 5 or 10, then use the rest of the number left. Eg, 6+7; use 4 of the 7 to get to 10, then you have 3 left which then = 13. If you are sitting on an 8; then you should know that you are 3 more than the last five and 2 away from the next 10.

Another goal of the crossover technique is to see and learn numbers relationship and perspective with a 5 or 10, which then reinforces this concept with all numbers. Visualization on My Pattern is key to lock in these thoughts forever. As everything in math, it helps greatly to see how this works on My Pattern or Game.

Multiplication:

Once the student gets to multiplication, it brings up some anxiety in what is coming next and how will they be able to master such a complicated concept. When starting, multiplication should be broken down to its basic form so that it is logical to the child/ student. It is really nothing more than a different or advanced way of counting and adding. It can be thought of simply as a way to count and add much more quickly. The child is using their own brain as a type of calculator or computer to make much faster additions.

At the very basic, multiplying is nothing more than a short cut to counting: Counting a one ten times equals = 1x10. Counting by 2's, counting by 5's, and counting by 10's are other ways to show how multiplication works. Therefore, multiplication should not be just putting 2 numbers together separated by an "x", and come up with a memorized answer.

What does it mean when you put 2 numbers together with an "x"? It often is very scary, but the child should be taught all of the ways to look at such a formula, and not simply be taught "multiplication tables". Given the simple problem: 2 x 3; this can demonstrate multiplication principles.

As in doing addition, in multiplication it helps to choose a reference number, and then the other number will be used to determine how many times it will repeat (multiple). So 2 x 3 can be written: 3 + 3; as there are #2 – 3s (=6). However, you can consider it as: 3 x 2; can be written: 2 +2+2 as there are #3 – 2s (=6). The answer will be the same whether done one way or the other. The child/ student will also learn which way works best for them. As you can also see, by writing this out, the rules and principles of each number and addition can be utilized.

The child should be allowed to look at these numbers and formula's and write out different ways they can be looked at. Also, it helps so much to use a visual pattern or grid. I will go over several different numbers to further demonstrate the rules and prinicples of multiplication.

Let's start with one (1). Any number times one is itself. For example, 4 x 1 = 4; which means that there is #1 – 4. The other way to say look at it is that there are #4 – 1s. Even something like 50 x1, means there are #1-50, or #50 – 1s. So, any formula of multiplication means that you can count one side or the other. For example: 2x3 means that you can count #2-3s, or #3-2s.

Next, let's go to the twos (2s). One of the most basic things is to count by 2s. 2, 4, 6, 8, 10, 12, etc… Counting by 2s is the same thing as multiplication, and the basis of multiplication tables. 2x1 is 2, which means there are #1 – 2, or there are #2-1s. Going on up, #2-2s (2x2) = 4; #3 – 2s (3x2) = 6, etc… One aspect of multiplying by 2 means that the other number is doubled. The other way to think about it is that the number multiplied by 2 is ½ or the answer. For example: 2 x 25 = 50; which means that 25 is ½ of 50. The other aspect of 2, is that every multiple of 2 is an even number. If it is an odd number, then it is not a multiple of 2.

Eg, 2 x 9: You can count #2 – nines, or you can count #9 – twos. If you use #2 – nines, then you can add 9+9, or consider the answer is a multiple of 9 and can simply go to the second multiple. If you use #9 – twos, then you can add the 2s together, or count by twos for 9 counts (=18).

We have already talked about multiples of 5 and 10 and how they can be used as a reference for all other numbers. Children learn to count by 5s and 10s, but be sure the child continues to think of this when doing multiplications of 5 and 10. How many times do you count by 5s in order to get to a certain multiple of 5? How many times do you count by 10s in order to get to a certain multiple of 10? For example: 25 is a multiple of 5, and you can get there if you count by 5s – five times, or multiplied by 5; or 5x5=25. Eg, 60 is a multiple of 10, which is reached by counting by 10 six times, or if multiplied by 6; or 10x6=60. It is also a multiple of 5, which means it got there by counting by 5s – 12 times; or 5x12 =60.

Multiples of the other numbers work the same way. Start by counting by that number, and then see where those numbers are on a visual pattern. Remember that if you are on a multiple, that you got there by multiplying by another number. Also, look at what each number is time 5 and times 10. These give you a reference point

-   Multiples of 3: 3, 6, 9, 12, 15 (x5), 18, 21, 24, 27, 30.
-   Multiples of 4: 4, 8, 12, 16, 20 (x5), 24, 28, 32, 36, 40
-   Multiples of 6: 6, 12, 18, 24, 30 (x5), 36, 42, 48, 54, 60
-   Multiples of 7: 7, 14, 21, 28, 35 (x5), 42, 49, 56, 63, 70
-   Multiples of 8: 8, 16, 24, 32, 40 (x5), 48, 56, 64, 72, 80
-   Multiples of 9: 9, 18, 27, 36, 45 (x5), 54, 63, 72, 81, 90

Then, by reviewing all of this, and using over and over again on a grid or playing a game, you will be able to see the multiples automatically.

From here, then the student will then probably get taught multiplication tables and the traditional way of multiplying larger numbers using columns. It is probably necessary, but should not be done without the child totally understanding what he/she is doing. The child should not be memorizing random tables and problems without understanding the principles.

Using a visual pattern or **Nelson's Train Stops** is even more important with multiplication. Look at the 2s all the way up to 100. Look at the 5s, 10s, and 20s. By seeing all of these numbers and results, and having a visual perspective makes all of math so much easier. You can also see all of this on my pattern or the Nelson's Train Stops.

Division:

Division probably induces more anxiety among children, as it looks complicated and can be at times. There are a few ways to look at division, and best to understand all of them. As adding and subtraction are opposites, so is division and multiplication, however, in a little different way.

I will try to give some basic concepts of what division means, even though more complicated division will be outside my scope here. I hope the basics at least make sense. Again, the child should understand the next steps very clearly, or they will quickly get frustrated. We already used some of the same principles.

One way to look at division is simply that it is a way to divide things up equally. Let's start simple. If you have one apple and you have one person, then you don't have to divide this up. It is 1 / 1 which is 1. So any number you divide by 1 is the same number, because you don't have to divide it up. 1 apple divided by 1 person = 1. So if there are 2 apples and still one person, those 2 apples don't have to be divided up. So, the answer is still 2. 2 apples for 1 person (2 / 1 = 2).

If there are still 2 apples but then for 2 persons, then you would need to divide them up, and divide up equally, so each person gets 1 apple. So 2 apples for 2 people = 1 (for each) (2 -:2 = 1). From there, you can use this concept to expand to the unlimited number of ways division can work. Use toothpicks, coins, or anything to demonstrate to your child. 4 apples for 2 people – 2 (for each) (4 / 2 = 2). 6 coins / 2 = 3; 10 coins divided by 5 (= 2) ; 20 coins / 4 (= 5); 20 coins / 5 (= 4).

This can then be used on a visual pattern, "My Pattern", or Nelson's Train Stops. Find the number you are starting with (eg, 10), then if it divided by 2, then you know it is in 2 parts, which is 5. If you are on 30 and you want to divide by 3, then divide it into 3 parts, and each part is 10. Also, go to 100 and divide by 5, and see that each part is 20.

The way division is opposite of multiplication is that the numbers in the formula are interchangeable. If you multiply 3 x 2 = 6, then dividing 6 by 2 = 3, and 6 by 3 = 2. Therefore, once you learn multiplication tables, then you can use those tables to reverse them in division. By learning these with the visual on a pattern, then they can easily be reversed. Part of the multiplication learning process is to learn what the multiples are of the different numbers, and what they look like. For example, given a number: 63, you should learn as part of visualizing multiplication, what the multiples are for 63. So, if you divide by 7, then you also know that the answer is 9. Did you notice that 6 + 3 = 9, so you knew that 63 was a multiple of 9.

Another way to demonstrate division is to identify the mulitples of numbers that are being divided. Let's look at dividing a number by 2. Start by looking at the multiples of 2 (2, 4, 6, 8, and 10). As you can see, it takes 5 – 2s to get to 10, so dividing 10 / 2 = 5; and 10 / 5 = 2.

If you didn't notice, the answer and the second number (divide by) are interchangeable. If you divide 30 / 10 = 3; then 30 / 3 =10. Another way to think about it, is that 30 can be divided up into #10 – 3s; or divided up into #3 – 10s.

Dividing by 2 means that you are taking the number and cut it in half. You are taking the initial number and splitting it into 2 equal parts. If the starting number is an even number, then it is easy. However, if an odd number, then it would create a fraction or a decimal. Any number with a 0 can be divided by 2, but it could end up with a 5 or 0 at the end. If the 10s digit is an odd number, then it will end in a 5 (eg, 30 / 2 = 15) if the 10s digit is an even number, then the answer will end in 0 (40 / 2 = 20).

Dividing by 3 means you split into 3 equal parts. Each part is then 1/3 or a "third". For the answer is to be a whole number, then it must be a multiple of a 3.

Dividing by 4 means you split into 4 equal parts. Each part is then ¼ or a "fourth" of the original number. It must be a mulitple of 4 in order to end up with a whole number.

Dividing by 5 or 10 means that you must be on a 5 or a 10 for the answer to be a whole number. However, this can easily be seen on my pattern. A multiple of a five will end in a 5 or a 0 in the one's column, and a 10 will end in a 0.

Dividing by 6, 7, 8, and 9 is the same as above. Know the multiples of each and what the corresponding division would look like. Remember, any number that can be divided by 9 will have all of there digits adding up to 9 or multiple of 9.

You may have noticed that that dividing is the same as multiplying a fraction. Unfortunately, I won't get into fractions here, but wanted to point this out.

Again, knowing all of the multiples of the above numbers while observing all of this on a visual pattern or ***Nelson's Train Stops***, will help you to understand and ingrain all of this into the memory.

More Math:

Above are my basics of mathematics for addition, subtraction multiplication, and division. However, there are so many other aspects that are outside the scope of this book. If this is successful, maybe I can expand the scope to include more aspects of mathematics. Those would include: Fractions, Powers, Squares and Square Roots, Logorithms, Algebra, Geometry, Triginometry, Calculus, Physics, and Statistics.

I wrote this with the idea of presenting my own techniques for numbers and math. The next book will probably require some collaboration with someone who knows what they are doing. ☺

CHAPTER 6

Summary & Personal Reflections

Personal Reflections-

I am not a math expert, but just someone who has used numbers and math extensively throughout my life. Logically, someone with much more expertise and knowledge in math than me should be writing such a book. Surely they know more than I do on how best to approach math and numbers. There may be other similar books available that give a different or better approach.

However, the reason I wrote this book and invented my game (***Nelson's Train Stops***) is only because other people, including teachers, thought my approach was somewhat unique and might be valuable to others. There also continues to be a large number of children who are not performing well in math. I don't have personal knowledge of why that is, but there is obviously something lacking.

One interesting thing is that you hear stories of children that have very poor math skills, but then are followed by stories of children who are excelling in school and math. What is the difference? What is the difference in what children are taught, learn, and understand? What is the difference in their approach, methodology, and skills in math? Is it possible that children that excel learn the appropriate perspectives and relationships of numbers and math, and either learn or develop their own methods and skills? Maybe children who are "bad" at math don't get the right instructions and don't learn perspectives and relationships of numbers and methods and skills of math. It appears that this needs to be studied to determine the "root cause" for these discrepencies. My premise is that all children need to know and learn all of the perspectives and methods within this book, along with some type of a visual tool to guide them in all aspects of numbers and math.

A critic might argue that not everyone could learn this type of approach. This is so unique that it really isn't going to help anyone else, or possibly just a few. However, there are other things I've seen that made me think this might be learned by and helpful to others.

I watched a 60 minutes (CBS) story one Sunday about a young male adult who is a "savant". The definition of a savant is *a person of* learning; *especially: one with detailed knowledge in some specialized field (as of science or literature) (**Webster Dictionary**).* He had difficulty with many activities of his life, but had incredible number and math skills. He could quickly do complicated mathematics computations in his head in 1-2 seconds. But the thing that struck home with me was that he visualized a different character for every single number. Each number would look totally different, just like a person would. This was part of what he saw when he was doing math. Therefore, he used a very strong visual to at least assist him with numbers and math. While watching this, I realized that I did something very similar. I don't see a different character, but I do see the number on "My Pattern", and use it to do math.

In the movie *"Rainman"*, Dustin Hoffman portrayed a type of a savant, who also was autist (I don't know if this always occurr concurrently). If you saw the movie, you remember how remarkable his numbers and math skills were. He could tell you what day of the week you were born, multiply large numbers in his head, and other amazing feats

Another 60 minutes story was the remarkable memory of Marilu Henner (Actress - *Taxi*) who has what is called: Highly Superior Auto-Biographical Memory, or H-SAM, which allows her to recall events in her life in incredible detail. She describes how others can learn to better use their memory, and uses a type of visualization to do so. http://newyork. cbslocal.com/2012/05/01/seen-at-11-rare-mental-condition-gives-actress-henner-super-human-memory/

Another 60 minute special documented that music has definitely been shown to improve learning. A recent Dana Report from Harvard documented similar results again. Music involves counting and math. Learning math should be like reading music. Following a pattern gives a reference point to a base for counting and computing math problems. It causes you to visualize the patterns and levels that are learned.

When I hear about children that have poor math skills, I wonder why and how they are able then to excel at other things. What are they doing differently that they are not doing in math?

Sports - Children demonstrate an incredible ability to excel in sports, even at a very early age. It seems that children often will learn more skills in the sport they are participating in than in math and reading in school. Any child in an orgainized league, especially in elite sports programs, will get lots of very specific instructions on "skills". Let's take baseball. They are not just told to go out and "play" baseball, without extensive and explicit instruction. To throw a ball: spread your feet, turn your shoulders, take the ball way behind your head, step toward your target, turn your shoulders, throw your ball, and follow through. That is just one skill necessary to play baseball. Can you imagine any athlete not doing repeated practice? Lee Trevino said that anyone can be a professional golfer; all you need to do is hit 500 golf balls a day. Maybe there should be a similar philosophy for math.

Golf is an example of a very difficult sport to master. I watched golf on television for years, but yet still would miss very specific but necessary skills to use with my golf swing. However, others can watch what they do, and pick up everything. Therefore, some need extra assistance and a different approach to master a sport and math.

Languages can be difficult to learn, but children who learn a different language early, seem to pick it up easily. However, learning a different language, requires a person to become engrossed in the language, and spend lots of time with the language, and understand what they are saying and hearing. Therefore, if any subject is difficult, then the child or student must be able to get the basic understanding, and then engross themselves in the subject.

Music is learned by becoming absorbed into it, otherwise, it is just playing a bunch of notes. Those children that do play an instrument well learn the music; understand what they are trying to do, get a "feeling" for the music, and practice, a lot. Is your child doing that in math? One of my references has demonstrated that children that play an instrument, do better in school, including math.

Learning Medicine is similar to learning a different language. I was fortunate to be able to start learning medicine as a pharmacist, but then once in medical school, I thought about very little else except medicine through medical school and residency. That is how doctors (and other professionals) become so knowledgeable, because they become engrossed in the subject.

Technology - children pick up on and excel in technology so early. Why is there not more use of technology to teach math. I started my children with "Math Blaster" 27 years ago.

Math as part of life: The way for a child to be engrossed in math and numbers is to make them a part of every day life. Games are a great way to learn and have fun, but it may not be enough. If the child plays numbers/math games and then never use any concepts until the next time they play, the child may not have the concepts ingrained into their memory. Somehow, they need to incorporate the concepts into their everyday life.

There needs to be a life relevance to every thing you do in math: Growing up and even today, when I come across any opportunity, I revert to my numbers and math memory. "Understanding Numbers" – should also be part of what the student is trying to accomplish. The student needs to learn to think "Numbers and Math". Use every opportunity to use these concepts. Are you taking a trip? How far away is your destination? How long will it take to travel there? How much gasoline will it take? What are your miles per gallon for the trip? Children should incorporate math into their everyday life.

Summary:

That completes my explanation of my philosophy and my approach to numbers and math. Whew! This was more than I had anticipated, and much harder to put down on paper than I had anticipated. I hope this wasn't too much, as I want to convey most of what I know or have thought about. I tried to remember and come up with the practical aspects and pointers that I used throughout my life. Hopefully it has been helpful to you.

There are 4 more sections that I decided to put at the end as appendices. They are related, but I couldn't figure out how to incorporate into above.

Appendix A: A brief summary of my philosophy and principles of numbers and math as I outlined above. This might help as a quick reference as reminders for the child and parent.

Appendix B: ***Nelson's Train Stops*** is a game I invented in conjunction with this book and refer to throughout the book. I actually invented this game before, but thought that I would release after I finished this book. Therefore the game gave me an incentive to finish this book sooner rather than later. The game displays many skills and tools that I talk about above. It displays the visualization that I saw and used throughout my life. However, the most important aspect is to play the game over and over again, to leave a permanent imprint of the visual on the young mind. The appendix is the section from the game that I give instructions to the parents.

Appendix C: This is the research that I did for this book, even though it didn't change what I wrote about my philosophy and methods above. All of the above is what I do and have done. The research is what I found while writing this book. But it supports what I do, and what else is available for the interested and motivated reader. I intentially did not do a lot of research before writing the book as I wanted to be totally original. However, I enjoyed doing the research and think that you should at least review the appendix to see the extensive work being done in the name of teaching children math. I also found that much of the research supports my philosophy and my methods. I even found research that supports my contention that board games improve math skills. Hopefully, all of that will help you and your children.

Appendix D: Some fun facts I came across in writing this book and doing some research.

Where we go from here:
Teachers:

This is not intended to replace what teachers already teach. In fact you notice I don't try to teach the usual methods for math: for example putting the numbers in columns for adding and subtracting, and multiplication, then to use brackets for division. All of these are and will still be necessary. My purpose is to give a child or student a different (maybe better) way to think about numbers, and to understand better what they are doing when they perform traditional math. Nor is this intended to be a criticism of teachers in any way. I am certainly not in a position to do that. Hopefully, this will be another tool they can use as part of their armentarium of teaching every day.

Parents:

This book is also in no way intended to be a criticism of parents. The point is to be pro-active in your child's education, of which most parents are. Also, it is important to find what works for every individual child. Monitor you child's progress closely, and talk and work with your child. Start numbers and math very early, and utilize my philosophies as above. Encourage using lots of math activities and games. Hopefully, you will find Nelson's Train Stops Game as a useful and fun tool. You might also think of your child as a "math athlete", and he/she may require lots of training and others maybe not so much.

Children/ Students:

Teach them to be pro-active in their own education. Be sure they understand all of these principles very early and encourage them to be responsible for their own learning. Show them how they can use numbers and math frequently in their daily lives. Teach them that it isn't bad if they don't understand something, and sometimes more education or a different kind of education is necessary.

Conclusion:

This is what I think about and have done my entire life and have demonstrated some proficiency in numbers and math. Hopefully, this has been beneficial to you as a teacher, parent, or child/student, and gives you a new, different, and possibly better perspective on how to approach numbers and math.

There are other approaches that are working for children, especially for those children that do excel at math. However, my approach may be benefecial for many. The key is "visualization" of a pattern such as the one I use and find beneficial. If I make even a small impact in the education of a child, I will feel that this was a success. See the appendices for further information and a list of some valued research.

Nelson's Train Stops is a compliment to this book and recommended for a young child at several different levels. It should be available by the publishing date of this book.

END

APPENDIX A

Brief Summary of Philosophies and Principles of Numbers and Math

Basic Premise of Book:

All of the principles taught in this book and the other important principles of numbers and math can be taught and learned by everyone.

Philosophy: Below summarizes my philosophies for numbers and math. Each philosophy is important to learn to truly learn and understand numbers and math. However, starting with number one (visualization) first and learning in order is best. Each requires the one before in order to take full advantage of my method.

1. **Visualization** – Visualization is the key to my entire approach. It is what makes all of it come together. However, visualization must have a pattern with a purpose and a plan.

2. **Relationship / Perspectives**: Use the visualization to learn how the entire number spectrum fits together. Taking any number and knowing how it relates to any other number or set of numbers allows the child to understand the relationships of numbers to other numbers and perspectives of number locations and how problems work and how to handle math problems. If they understand this first, the next steps at least make sense. Otherwise, they are just random numbers without any meaning.

3. **Principles, Rules, and Skills**: Once the understanding is there, then the child needs to learn all of the principles, rules, and skills. Learning the ones that I presented above, plus others, will allow

the student to be an active participant, instead of just trying to memorize charts and formulas. Think of this in terms of a sport that requires learning lots of skills.

4. **Repetition:** Once you master the first three, then all that is left is repetition. However, children need an incentive to have repetition, and to "practice", similar to any sport. My goal in creating ***Nelson's Train Stops*** is to find something the child may find fun and interesting to want to play "repeatedly". This should only be the beginning.

Rules and Principles of Numbers: The above book explains this in great detail.

One (1) is the most basic number. It is like counting forward (addition) and counting backwards (subtraction). Multiplying or dividing a1 results in no change in the number.

Two (2): can be thought of as counting 2 times up or down. Counting by 2s, you can then see where all of the even numbers are. If not a multiple of 2, then it is considered an odd number.

Three (3): 3 is 3 more than zero, but 2 less than 5. You can count by 3 to see the multiples.

Four (4): 4 is 4 more than zero, but 1 less than 5. It is common to use this perspective to add and subtract.

Five (5) & Ten (10): Know the rule of 5s and 10s. These are common to use as reference points. When adding or subtracting, know if it is crossing a 5 or 10, then use the crossover technique. Remember that every number has a relationship with 5 and 10. Know the multiples of 5 and 10, and that any number ending in 5 or 10 is a multiple of 5, and those ending in 10 is a multiple of 10.

Six (6): 6 is 1 more than 5. It is easy to use 5 then add or subtract a 1.

Seven (7): 7 is 2 more than 5, but 3 less than 10. Either perspective can be used.

Eight (8): 8 is 3 more than 5, but 2 less than 10. Either perspective can be used.

Nine (9): 9 is 4 more than 5, but 1 less than 10. It is common to use 10, then add or subtract a 1.

All other numbers: have their own principles and rules as reviewed in detail above.

Rules and Principles of Math:

Addition: start by counting. Often, you can simply know the answer, just by knowing the principles of the number(s).

Subtraction: like counting backwards. Often, you can simply know the answer, just by knowing the principles of the number(s).

CrossOver Technique: Used with 5 and 10. Know how far to the next 5 or 10, then use part of the number to get there, then the rest to go to the other side.

Multiplication: Similar to adding, but adding multiples of the same number. See the multiples on a pattern, and learn where they are.

Division: Several ways to look at. It is essentially dividing a number into a smaller part. Dividing a number by 2 is the same as ½. Dividing by 3 is the same as 1/3. Knowing multiplication tables will give you answers for division. Eg, 2 x 3 = 6; 6 / 2 = 3; 6 / 3 = 2.

Visualization: of all of the principles for numbers and math on a pattern or a grid is essential and my first "philosophy". Viewing this pattern will allow the child to "see" and remember the rules and principles just by viewing this pattern, and then can remember in their memory. View all Principles of Numbers and Math on *Nelson's Train Stops.*

APPENDIX B

Nelson's Train Stops: A Numbers and Math Game

In the process of writing this book, I came up with a game that follows my numbers pattern and how I have utilized numbers throughout my life. This game utilizes all of the principles that I believe necessary for numbers and math learning for a lifetime. It utilizes a very useful pattern. It gives the child a visualization, shows many rules and principles of numbers and math, and is hopefully fun for children to play repetitively, especially the young child. It involves many things that children love: bears, trains, and mountains. All children love bears and trains.

Instead of trying to re-write an entire section, below is a reprint of the supplemental instructions booklet that I include with the game that is directed to the parents of children playing the game. The parents can then be aware of the goals the games is trying to accomplish and can be "helpful" for the children. It has 5 different levels to allow for the very young child (2 years of age, and maybe younger), all the way up to age 8 to 10. I believe it is possible for the child to start very young and possibly progress very fast if he/ she really enjoys the game and learning everything the game has to offer. The game includes the basic instructions on how to play and the supplemental instructions for parents as written below.

The below section repeats many of the same things already covered and refers back to the contents of the book above. However, you can see the general principles for the game itself and how it might be very beneficial for a child you know. I also believe that it might be beneficial for older children, adolescesces, young adults, and possibly older adults, or anyone that might struggle with math and don't have a system for numbers and math.

Nelson's Train Stop: **Principles & Philosophy: A Supplement for Parents**

The game may not look much different from a lot of other board games. This game was designed as a game first and a learning game second. The goal is to make the game fun, then add some number and math education as they play and move up to different levels. All children love trains. We hope the children will love the lay out and the way the game is played.

The philosophy and principles of the Game is outlined below. These will give you some information on how best to use the Game and get the most out of it. This supplement is designed for the parent(s) and to share important points with their children. As they get older and/or advance, the parent will want to share more and more of this information. However, if the child is able to read and comprehend the contents of this and my book, then this will certainly give the child a sense of accomplishment and self sufficiency.

These closely coincide with all of the information outlined in my book: *"Making Sense of Numbers and Math"*, which goes into much more detail. I would recommend for all parents and children able to read.

My Philosophy of Learning Math:

My overriding philosophy of Learning Math and the Game is very simple: any child or person can learn to be good at Math; they only need the tools necessary to accomplish that goal. How do some children excel at Math, yet others don't. I believe it comes down to three basic reasons. One is that some children have an inate ability to learn and use math and numbers, while others do not. Two, our educational system does not appear to be reaching those children that don't have that inate ability. Finally, I believe that children commonly don't incorporate math and numbers into their everyday life. They are learning math and numbers in school and learn what they need to do. They then go home, may do their homework, but only do what is required, without any further thought about math or numbers. Nelson's Train Stops is just one more thing that gives them the opportunity to use math in a fun way, and gives them supplemental information and tools they can assist them in their learning.

The goal is for the child / children to use these philosophies and principles in their daily use of math and numbers. Math is logical and always makes sense. The child may need to learn what that is.

I explain this even further in my book: *"Making Sense of Numbers and Math"*. I also explain that I am not a math teacher or mathemetician. Therefore, I don't pretend to know as much or more than they do. I am only giving my philosophy and introduce some new tools on how to learn math. Given the state of childhood math skills in this country, this could be of great help.

The Goals for *Nelson's Train Stops*:

The main goal of "**Nelson's Train Stops**" is to provide children or students a fun way to learn and to utilize my four philosophies of learning numbers and math. These include: **Visualization, Relationships/ Perspective, Principles and Rules, and Repetition.**

- **Visualization** is so important in working with numbers. Given a lone number, without any other numbers to compare it to is rather worthless. Children playing on a board game visualizes any given number while instantly comparing it to all other numbers and where it falls in the whole spectrum of numbers. They begin to formulate in their minds a visualization pattern without being forced to do so. Visualization has been proven to improve learning (see references in Appendix C). Every number on this board will have a permanent place in your child's brain. When ever he/she hears a number from 0 to 100, he/she will visualize the number.

- **Relationships/ Perspective**: Part of visualization, is seeing the relationship of all numbers and how they look in comparison to the others. In other words a geographical map of numbers: the total map, the starting point, the roadmap with directions, and the final destination. Eg, the number 50 seems like a nonspecific number without significance by itself. But seeing it on *Nelson's Train Stops*, the child easily sees it is the halfway point between 0 and 100. Being close to 50 is close to being halfway. They also see it is a multiple of 5 and 10.

o   The distance in relation to the final destination. For example if you go from 0 to 5, the child actually sees how much further he/she has to go.

o   When adding or subtracting, the child will be able to visualize on the board (then later in the mind). The child may have to count at first, but then will see what it looks like to have to move a certain number of spaces. (Eg, Add 3 to 4, he/she can easily see the 3 spaces and not have to count).

-   **Principles and Rules:** Children may play games and use numbers and math, but don't think to use appropriate principles. It is important to learn the principles of numbers then those of math, even though there is significant overlap. It is similar to playing a sport. A child may have talent, but if not shown the fundamentals of that sport (eg, a golf swing or throwing a ball), he/she may not truly grasp what they are supposed to do. Even if a child has a knack for numbers and math, learning the principles will allow him/her to be even better.

-   **Repetition**: The reason we hope to make the game fun, is to encourage children to play often. It is also another reason that we developed several levels, so children won't get bored. The more they play the game, especially if no pressure or stress, the more they will learn and remember.

Finally, my goal and theory is, after the child has played this game many times, will have a permanent visual memory of each number on the Game Board. This also includes how to have a permanent visual memory of all numbers, to infinity. This is explained further in the book: *"Making Sense of Numbers and Math"*.

Principles and Rules: For the Game and Thereafter:

Problem Solving:

Before performing math problems, it is important to understand numbers first. I discussed my philosophies above, however it is helpful to review before moving on, and frequently refer back to. Sometimes, there is the assumption that when a topic is learned once, then going back to that information is not necessary. All information, starting at 1+1, needs to be readily available to go back to review and reinforced. Make sure the child knows he/she can always go back to look something up, without feeling bad about it.

So remember the four philosophies: visualization, relationship/ perspective, principles/rules, and repetition. Performing math problems needs to follow the same or similar process every time. Math teachers require students to show their work for the same reason. Each move of the Game therefore, should follow the same principle.

With each move the Player performs a Math problem. The Player needs to perform each problem in his/her head and then make the move. Initially, the Player may need to use a separate piece of paper to perform the computations. However, the Game Board itself can be used as an "aide". If done enough, the child will remember the Board and the process and perform computations much easier.

Therefore, the purpose of the Game and Board is to help the child to always have a visual of what they are doing while playing the game. Even if using the spinner, Level I, the child will be "adding" to where they are. They may count at first, but then later asked to "do the Math".

The Board Layout and Purpose:

On first glance, the board doesn't look any different than most Board type games. However, I will highlight the important aspects. It is a set of trains and train stations on a railroad track that goes through a scenic route through the mountains. This should attract the attention of children as they are commonly attracted to trains and bears (Nelson).

The numbers are on the tracks between rails and go from 1 to 100. Again, this isn't unusual, but there is a purpose behind this number. If the child can master all of the numbers and math computations from 1 to 100, then he/she can apply it to all numbers as I will explain later.

In the middle of the board is a large train station and is the number 50. This already gives the child the immediate perspective that 50 is halfway to 100. The Train Stations are set every 10 spaces. This immediately gives the child the perspective of how the 10s look and are spaced. They can see a "visual" of the perspective.

The Trains are on the numbers that end in "5". By combining the trains and the train stations, the child easily sees multiples of 5s, and can see the perspectives and the relationships between the 5s, 10s, and the other numbers. What's amazing to see, is how few numbers there are that are not 5s or 10s. There are only 4 numbers that occur between each multiple of 5.

The route starts slow, with the numbers 1-10 to be larger and very prominent, but still in perspective of the rest of the Board. Learn and know and Perspective of 1-10.

There are only 8 numbers from 1-10 that isn't a 5 or a 10. Each number 1-4, and 6-9 has its own relationship with 5 and 10. By recognizing this relationship means the child knows the relationship to infinity.

For example, 1 is always 1 more than 0 but means 11 is one more than 10, and so on. But it is also 4 less than 5. 2 is 3 less than 5; 3 is 2 less than 5; and 4 is one less than 5. If one automatically knows that, then, computations can be done automatically. In other words, adding 3 to 4 means that getting to 5 leaves 2 more. Then by knowing 7 is always 2 more than 5, the answer is automatic, but not necessarily memorized. The numbers 6-9 have a perspective with 5 and 10. So, the child should learn how much each is above 5 and below 10. One could use either during any computation. In other words, adding 6 to 8 means it took 2 to get to 10, and that leaves 4 left, which then gives 14 as the answer.

- Adding 5 or 10 to any number means that the same perspective is kept with a computation. Eg. Adding 5 to 8: 8 is 3 more than 5, so adding 5 means that the answer is 3 more than 10 = 13. Adding 10 to 7: keep the same perspective as in the 1-10 numbers= 17.

- All of this is easily seen throughout the entire Game Board. However, periodically, the parent may need to show or remind the child.

- Nelson's Train Stops only goes up to 100, which limits its scope somewhat. However, the purpose of this game is to give a foundation for using the principles for all numbers, up into the hundreds, thousands, millions, and on up to infinity. The goal is to develop future games that apply those principles to much higher numbers.

These are further explained with my book: ***"Making Sense of Numbers and Math"***.

Addition:

The first thing the child will do, at Level I, is to use the spinner, land on a number, then move forward that many spots. Certainly, the child should start by counting forward, or "steps". However, at some point, the parent might suggest that the child take the number and "add" it to where they are currently located (or subtract if so instructed). This requirement can be added to the game as a requirement at any point.

Certainly, if the players/ children are at Level III, then you should consider prohibiting counting, even though you should allow visualizing the board.

Each number has its own principles or rules. The same rules can be used for both addition and subtraction. Subtraction should be thought of as addition, only in reverse. This is the same for multiplication and division (discussed later). More information is in my book: ***"Making Sense of Numbers and Math"***.

Subtraction:

There will be a back button on the spinner and there will be subtraction cards that the child will have to use. Beginners (Level I) will start by counting backwards. This will give the child a visual of what subtracting looks like.

However, the children should learn how to do the subtraction as soon as possible. As above with additions, at some point, the children should not be allowed to count but to use the principles to do the subtraction and then move the piece to the new spot. More information is in my book: ***"Making Sense of Numbers and Math"***.

Multiplication:

As we get into Levels III, IV and then V, multiplication problems will be added. The player/ child will take the card and be required to compute a problem and then use it in the game.

Initially, the problem will be quite simple, but then the problem may be a level 2 problem. For example, multiply 2x3 and add that to your current location and move to that spot.

There will be some limit to using multiplication and division as the final destination is 100. Continue to emphasize the basic principles of addition and multiplication. Multiplication is nothing more than adding multiples of numbers together.

Eg., Multiplying 2x3 is nothing more than adding #2 – 3s together, or adding #3 – 2x together. This can be easily visualized on the board and helps to make multiplication make more sense. More informatin is in my book: *"Making Sense of Numbers and Math".*

Divisions:

As in multiplication, division will be introduced slowly starting at Level III, and then more advanced in Level IV and V. The player/ child will take the card and be required to compute a problem and then use it in the game. Initially it will be simple, then gradually more advanced. Level V will have 2 step questions requiring a computation and then application to the Game.

Division can be looked at as either subtraction of multiples of a number; or it can be looked at as a reverse of multiplication. More information is in my book: *"Making Sense of Numbers and Math".*

Basic Rules of 5s and 10s –

Numbers 1-10 each have their own set of principles, rules, and shortcuts. Those rules can then be extrapolated to all numbers. Since my Game Board emphasizes the multiples 5 and 10, I want to elaborate a little bit more on the Rules of 5s and 10s. These rules should be covered well in school, but I will give my explanation.

It is important to know where all of the 5s and 10s are and how to use them in computations. The Game Board highlights where the 5s (Trains) and the 10s (Stations) are and will assist anyone doing Math. If a number ends in 0, then it is always a multiple of 10. For the purpose of this Game and Board, it includes the numbers: 10, 20, 30, 40, 50, 60, 70, 80, 90, and 100, and is designated by a Train Station. Any time a number is added to a 10, then the digit on the right is always the same. This is the case for a number added to any multiple of 10; the right digit is always the same. This is also true because any multiple of 10 always has a 0 in the right column. For example, adding 8 to 10= 18. 13 + 10= 23.

But part of this is to know how all of the other numbers are in relation to the number 10 and multiples of 10. Knowing this helps in all computations. If a number ends in 0 or 5, then it is always a multiple of 5. These include 5, 10, 15, 20, 25, 30, etc. on up to 100. Any time a number is added to a 5, then the answer will have the same relationship with a multiple of 5. Eg. 9 is 1 less than 10 or 4 more than a multiple of 5. The answer (14) is also 1 less or 4 more than a multiple of 5. 18 is also 2 less than 20; so if you add 5, you know the answer will be 2 less than 25 which is 23.

Adding or subtracting a 5 or 10 will always put the new number in the same relationship as the old number. (Eg, 8 + 5= 13, 8+20= 28, etc.)

Other Rules:

In addition to the above, there are many other rules. Every number has its own rules and relationships, which includes its relationship with a multiple of 5 or 10. Knowing that relationship of any number or your spot in respect to the multiple of 5 or 10 is very important to assist in understanding numbers and performing Math problems.

- Other examples:
  o A multiple of 2 is always an "even" number. It always skips a number, which is the odd number. However if you start on an odd number, then adding 2 puts you on another odd number. There is always #5 2s within 10 spaces.
  o 3 is 3 more than a multiple of 5 (0), but 2 less than a multiple of 5. It is 3 more than (0), but 7 less than (10). The number 8 is similar to the 3 as it is 3 more than 5, but 2 less than 10. Also, 3 plus 5 equals 8. The number 13 then is 3 more than 10, 2 less than 15, and 7 less than 20. If you add the "digits" of any number and it comes to 3, then it is divisable by 3. For example, add the digits of 12 (1+2) = 3. Adding the digits of 39 (3+9) = 12, then 1+2=3.

Using the Game Board to visualize these concepts will reinforce these principles and will implant a permanent visualization for the child. More information is in my book: ***"Making Sense of Numbers and Math"***.

Final Comments:

Hopefully this (extra section) gives you (the parent) and the child the basic instruction with some extra ideas on how best to get the most out of the game. At least it gives you an idea of my thought processes on the development and goal of the game.

It may seem like a lot, but it is something the child can and should learn gradually after playing many times. I would venture to say that many "teens" are not aware of many of the things outlined and utilized here. Therefore, anything your child can gain from this is a plus.

There are so many aspects of math, hopefully, the child will enjoy all of the different aspects with the game, want to learn everything, and even come up with their own rules and tricks.

In other words, I hope that the child finds this type of game and learning math fun, for a long time.

And, of course, I also hope that you and your child/children will want to get more from my book: ***"Making Sense of Numbers and Math"***.

Endorsement and Teacher Guidance:

The contents of this game and my book were made possible by input by a certified secondary education teacher; who also gave her official endorsement of the final products.

APPENDIX C

Research and Current Math Learning Methods, Theories, and Controversies

I wanted to include a section on some research and current thinking on numbers and math education. In spite of the fact that math skills among American students is not what it should be, there continues to be a mind boggling amount of information written and studied on how best to teach our children numbers and math. So much is written about this topic and reasearch performed. This can be demonstrated simply by doing a Google search of: "Math Education", which then gives "approximately 421,000,000 results". Also, imagine that every university in the country has a mathematics department, each doing its own research, and each with Ph.D's doing research for their dissertation. Then add on all of the Math Societies, independent educators, and then all school districts nationwide trying to find everything written about it and the best way to teach our students.

Therefore, I don't intend for this to be a chapter of exhaustive research on mathematical education, however, provide a very small sample to give the reader a flavor of what types of information is available, and I believe it does that. It will also give the motivated reader, whether educator, parent, or student, a starting point to do their own research.

With all of this information and research, it is difficult to imagine why there is such a large problem with children learning math. There continues to be lots of controversy on the best way to teach math.

As I said in my introduction, my method is what worked very well for me, and I believe this or a similar system will work very well for others.

It seems that the below writings and research support the philosophy and skills taught with my method. At the very least, they do nothing to discredit anything I have recommended above. Therefore, maybe it is worth a try. It is possible that my methods have already been written about and/or studied; however, I have yet to see anything yet.

1.   **Theories of Mathematics Education,** Seeking New Frontiers
      Editors: B. Sriraman; L. English, 2010, 668pp, Hardcover
      ISBN: 978-3-642-00741-5
      http://www.springer.com/978-3-642-00741-5

This is an extensive 660 page textbook with 50+ contributing authors and reviews many aspects of mathematics education research. The book contains input from multi-generational math educators as far back as the 1960's when math research journals were first intitiated and from those from many different view points. I will try to provide some samples and points from the book.

To give you a flavor of the discussions, some of the chapter titles included: Surveying Theories and Philosophies of Mathematics Education, Reflections on Theories of Learning, On the Theoretical, Conceptual, and Philosophical Foundations for Research in Mathematics Education, Theories of Mathematics Education: Is Plurality a Problem?, Re-conceptualizing Mathematics Education as a Design Science, Concept Construction Underlying Various Theoretical Frameworks, Problem Solving for the 21st Century, Understanding a Teacher's Actions in the Classroom by Applying Schoenfeld's Theory.

The Introduction (A Synthesized and Forward-Oriented Case for Mathematics Education) states: "The book presents a good case that theory development is indeed progressing on different geographical and trans-disciplinary fronts, and our field has indeed consolidated and synthesized previous work and moved forward in unimagined and productive ways."

Of all chapters, I will briefly discuss the one chapter: "Reflections on Theories of Learning", by Paul Ernest. Below are exerpts directly from his summary: **"Implications for Educational Practice":**

"Ultimately, the importance of a learning theory concerns its implications for practice, both pedagogically, in the teaching (and learning) of mathematics, and in the practice of conducting educational research. However, in my view, there is little in any pedagogy that is either wholly necessitated or wholly ruled out by the other elements of a learning theory. Similarly, learning theories do not imply particular research approaches. Nevertheless, certain emphasis are foregrounded by different learning theories, even if they are not logical consequences of them.

Simple constructivism suggests the need and value for: (1) sensitivity towards and attentiveness to the learner's previous learning and constructions; (2) identification of learner errors and misconceptions and the use of diagnostic teaching and cognitive conflict techniques in attempting to overcome them.

Radical constructivism suggests attention to: (3) learner perceptions as a whole, i.e., of their overall experiential world, (4) the problematic nature of mathematical knowledge as a whole, not just the learner's subjective knowledge, as well as the fragility of all research methodologies.

Enactivism suggests that we attend to: (5) bodily movements and learning, including the gestures that people make, (6) the role of root metaphors as the basal grounds of learners' meanings and understanding.

Social constructivism places emphasis on:(7) the importance of all aspects of the social context and of interpersonal relations, especially teacher-learner and learner-learner interactions in learning situations including negotiation, collaboration and discussion, (8) the role of language, texts and semiosis in the teaching and learning of mathematics.

However, each one of these eight focuses in the teaching and learning of mathematics could legitimately be attended to by teachers drawing on any of the learning theories for their pedagogy, or by researchers employing one of the learning theories as their underlying structuring framework."

Summary of Book:

As you can see, the language is highly intellectual, and maybe teachers understand this the same way I understand medical language. However, I still wonder if there is some difficulty in taking the information presented in this type of textbook to the classroom, teachers, and ultimately to the students?

It appears that the author is trying to say that the instructor needs to be sensitive to the needs of the learner with attention to language, prior instruction and understanding, and how the student learns best. This follows my logic above in that standard teaching doesn't always reach all of the children. Children need to be able to learn their own way in order for them to truly understand what they are trying to learn and do.

2. **Mathematics Education: A Summary of Research, Theories, and Practice,** August, 2002, Thomson/ Nelson Publisher.

This book was found online and appears to have lots of practical information for teachers. It is relatively short (52 pages) and appears to be written by several authors on a web site sponsored by "Nelson Education LTD" (www.nelson.com). The organization and website states that its purpose is to support and disseminate information to teachers and educators thoughout Canada.

From the website: "Nelson Education Ltd. is Canada's leading educational publisher providing innovative products and solutions for learners of all ages. Nelson values and respects the life long learning continuum and dedicates its business efforts to the diverse learning needs of students and educators alike." Cengage Learning is a highly respected US academic & professional publisher."

The book is a practical application of research and theories for the education community, as it discusses the use of all of the principles presented for curriculum changes in Canada.

The most important chapter that I saw was: **Learning Mathematics; which includes:**

Problem Solving, Procedural Fluency, Mental Math and Estimation, Multiple Representations and Mental Imagery, Manipulatives, Reasoning and Reflecting, Communicating Mathematically, Appreciating Mathematics, and Learning Styles.

I found the section: Learning Styles was worth elaborating on, with the following exerpts: "All of the theories or models with respect to learning styles place the child at the centre of the learning process. They all emphasize that effective teaching occurs when children are given opportunities to learn in ways that maximize their strengths, while at the same time developing their less-preferred styles. All approaches stress the importance of making connections for students—connections between new learning and prior learning, between learning in one subject and learning in another, between what goes on in the classroom and the world beyond."

The chapter presented the "Four Categories of Learning Style "(Curry, 1987):

1. **Personality dimensions** address issues that deal with measures of extroversion/introversion, sensing/intuition, thinking/feeling, and judging/perception (Witkin, 1954 and Myers-Briggs, 1978); Information **processing** considers how the individual assimilates information. Kolb's (1984) "experiential learning cycle" is the best-known model in this category. It identifies fourphases of learning: concrete experience, reflective observation, abstract conceptualization, and active experimentation. **Social interaction** deals with the individual's interactions in the classroom. Reichmann and Grasha (1974) identified six types of learner: independent, dependent, collaborative, ompetitive, participant, and avoidant. **Instructional preference** addresses the individual's preferred learning environment. Central to this category is the model developed by Dunn and Dunn (1978), which led to the development of a Learning Styles Inventory (LSI) designed to aid educators in matching teaching environments to individual learner preferences."

(2) **Cultural differences:** A significant body of research has examined the extent to which learning style preferences are culturally determined. However, much of the research warns against making generalizations about the preferred learning styles of cultural groups as a whole. There exists diversity of learning style preferences in all cultures and wise use of our understanding about style preferences involves looking at each student as a unique individual.

(3) **Multiple Intelligences:** Howard Gardner (1989), by defining intelligence as "the capacity to solve problems or to fashion products that are valued in one or more cultural settings," has allied himself closely with earlier learning and cognitive style theorists. Gardner's multiple intelligences model (1983) questioned the view that intelligence is limited to reason, intellect, logic, and knowledge. He has proposed that there are at least eight intelligences—and

perhaps more—that include areas such as music, spatial relations, and interpersonal knowledge, as well as mathematical and linguistic intelligence. Gardner further maintains that everyone is born with these multiple intelligences but, depending on a multitude of factors, students come to school with these intelligences developed to varying degrees. He asserts that educators need to acknowledge the existence of multiple intelligences, to accept that students come to school with these intelligences developed to varying degrees, and be prepared to adjust curriculum, instruction, and assessment accordingly. Gardner's model does not advocate simply adapting program to each student's most highly developed intelligences. Rather, good instruction allows students not only to demonstrate their strengths but also to further develop those intelligences that are less dominant."

The rest of the book appears to have lots of other good discussions that would be of interest for the motivated reader. Some of the remaining chapters are: Teaching Mathematics, Assessment in Mathematics Education, Comparative Studies in Mathematics Education, Technology in Mathematics Education, and Home/School Connections.

Ironically, the website is www.nelson.com and the company is Nelson Publishing. I was not aware of this until long after I invented my game: ***Nelson's Train Stops.*** My use of Nelson comes from my middle name. This was also my late father's middle name and the name he went by, and therefore, it was dedicated to him. I also thought that Nelson was a cute name for a bear (see my children's book ***Nelson Learns Math***).

3. **APOS: A Constructivist Theory of Learning in Undergraduate Mathematics Education Research,** Ed Dubinsky, Georgia State University, USA, and Michael A. McDonald, Occidental College, USA.

The theory presented here begins with the hypothesis that mathematical knowledge consists in an individual's tendency to deal with perceived mathematical problem situations by constructing mental *actions*, *processes*, and *objects* and organizing them in *schemas* to make sense of the situations and solve the problems. In reference to these mental constructions we call it *APOS Theory*. The ideas arise from our attempts to extend to the level of collegiate mathematics learning the work of J. Piaget on reflective abstraction in children's learning.

Initially, this may not seem related to early childhood math learning. However, it follows my philosophy of contructing mental actions and processes, using objects, organizing them into schemas, to make sense of the situation and problems: very similar to what I discussed above.

4. **ScienceBlog:** Published in the Journal: ***Development Psychology;*** Elizabeth Gunderson, PhD, Univ of Chicago Postdoctoral scholar; Susan Levine, Professor in Psychology at Univ of Chicago. http://scienceblog.com/55020/learning-about-spatial-relationps-boosts-understanding-of-numbers/

Scholars at University of Chicago have shown that working with puzzles and learning to identify shapes are connected to improved spatial understanding and bettter achievement.

"They found that children's spatial skills at the beginning of first and second grades predicted improvements in linear number line knowledge over the course of the shool year." Dr. Gunderson. "These results suggest that improving children's spatial thinking at a young age may not only help foster skills specific to spatial reasoning butalso improve symbolic numerical representations." S. Levine.

Another reference that supports my principles and philosophies I presented above, and supports the benefits of a "numbers board game" such as: ***Nelson's Train Stops.***

5. **Theori**es of Mathematics Education: 2005. In Chick, H. L. & Vincent, J. L. (Eds.). *Proceedings of the 29th Conference of the International Group for the Psychology of Mathematics Education*, Vol. 1, pp. 170-202. Melbourne: PME. http://www.emis.de/proceedings/PME29/PME29ResearchForums/PME29RFEnglishSriraman.pdf

Essays by: Lyn English, Queensland University of Technology, Bharath Sriraman, The University of Montana; Frank K. Lester, Jr., Indiana University,

Bloomington, USA; Stephen Lerman, London South Bank University, UK; Luis Moreno Armella, Cinvestav, Mexico.; John Pegg, University of New England (Australia); David Tall, University of Warwick (UK); Richard Lesh, Indiana University (USA); Lyn English, Queensland University of Technology (Australia); Günter Törner, Duisburg-Essen Universität (Germany);

A series of six short essays on theories of mathemeatics education. It is very intellectual and probably appeals to educators in academics. Below is an exerpt from the the summary.

Summary of Publication (exerpt): (concluding points by the authors: Chick and Vincent)

"The diversity in the perspectives presented in the six contributions parallel conundrums recently elicited by Tommy Dreyfus at the 4th European Congress in Mathematics Education (Spain, February 2005). In his concluding report about the working group on mathematics education theories, Dreyfus stated that although theories were a vital aspect of mathematics education, they were much too wide of a topic. However the field can take solace from the fact that although contradictions exist, there are also connections and degrees of complementarities among theories. The coordinators of this particular Forum have reached a similar conclusion. Many of the points we make here echo the recommendations of Tommy Dreyfus. Although it is impossible to fully integrate theories, it is certainly possible to bring together researchers from different theoretical backgrounds to consider a given set of data or phenomena and examine the similarities and differences in the ensuing analysis and conclusions. The interaction of different theories can also be studied by applying them to the same empirical study and examining similarities and differences in conclusions. Last but not least, although it is impossible to expect everybody to use the mathematics education "language," a more modest undertaking would be to encourage researchers to understand one or more perspectives different from their own. This will ensure that the discussion continues as well as creates opportunities for researchers to study fruitful interactions of seemingly different theories. We consider such work vital to help move the field forward."

I included this in order to be complete and appeal to any math "experts". They do make the point that somehow results of research need to reach the classroom and not to form theories for academic purposes only.

6. Jean Piaget's Cognitive Development Theory in Mathematics Education, by Kristin E. Reedal, Department of Mathematics and Computer Science – Ripon College, published in **Summation:** May 2010, pp. 16-20, http://ripon.edu/macs/summation.

The paper discusses Jean Piaget's developmental stages and applies this theory to the learning of mathematics. More specially, this theory of learning will be applied to the concepts of one-to-one correspondence and comparisons. Jean Piaget's cognitive development theory discusses how an individual progresses through the learning process in stages. I find the article easy to follow and explains his theory better than prior articles sited. I will try to summarize, but it would be recommended to read the entire article to get a good full discussion of Piaget's Theory.

Piaget focuses his theory on the idea of constructivism, which is that learning is constructed from each individual's experiences and connections between previously learned concepts and new ideas [3]. This leads into his idea of disequilibrium, which drives the learning process. Piaget's theory of disequilibrium describes when new ideas and concepts do not fit with what we already know and therefore we are forced to adjust our thinking to incorporate this new information [2]. Finding how concepts are connected and fit together allows us to reach a point of equilibrium.

He presents his COGNITIVE DEVELOPMENT THEORY. Jean Piaget identifies four stages of cognitive development that all children will progress through at some point in their lives: (1) Sensorimotor Stage, (2) Pre-operational Stage, (3) Concrete Operations, (4) Format Operations.

The first stage of development that Piaget identifies is the Sensorimotor Stage. This is generally between birth and two years old, although children will progress through this stage at their own pace [9]. At this point, children are learning using their five senses and need concrete experiences to understand concepts and ideas [2]. Also at this stage, children are limited in their world and what they are able to comprehend. Children are egocentric and can only see the world from their own perspective [2]. He then addressed how the *Sensorimotor Stage* applies to mathematics; we can see how learning is developing.

Piaget believed that the amount of time each child spends in each stage of development will vary based on the individual [9]. Not all children will be at the same stage of development at same ages. So while each child will progress through the stages of development that Jean Piaget identifies, each child should be an active participant in this learning process."

Preoperational Stage: The second stage of cognitive development identified by Jean Piaget is the Preoperations Stage, during two to seven years old [2]. "During this period, children are able to do onestep logic problems, develop language, continue to be egocentric, and complete operations" [2]. These children's development continues, and this stage marks the beginning of solving more mathematically based problems like addition and subtraction.

Concrete Operations Stage: The next stage of development that Piaget discusses is the Concrete Operations Stage, which generally recognizes a child between the ages of seven to eleven years old [2]. A child would be able to think logically and start classifying based on several features and characteristics rather than solely focusing on the visual representation [9].

D. Formal Operations Stage: The last stage of development that Piaget identifies is the Formal Operations Stage, which children enter roughly between the ages of eleven to sixteen years old and continues throughout adulthood [10]. This marks the distinct change of a child's thinking to a more logical, abstract thinking process.

CONCLUSION: Overall Jean Piaget's Developmental theory allows us to see how a concept develops and outlines how a child progresses through this developmental process of learning. We can also see how topics are related and build off of each other, especially one-to-one correspondence and comparisons. Examining Piaget's theory begs the question of whether we are pushing students in our educational system through this developmental process too quickly and asking them to learn concepts before they are capable of fully understanding these ideas. This leads to the importance of determining where a child is before presenting new information to fully address whether a child is capable of understanding the new material based on their current developmental stage. So, understanding how a child moves through this developmental process can enhance our understanding of how children learn and therefore increase the chances of understanding new complex ideas. (Again, very consistent with my discussions in the main part of this book)

7. **An Overview of Theories of Learning in Mathematics Education Research**, an Essay by Jim Cottrill, June 2003.
   http://centroedumatematica.com/ciaem/articulos/universitario/
   conocimiento/An%20Overview%20of%20Theories%20of%20
   Learning%20in%20Mathematics%20Education%20Research.%20
   2003*Cottril,%20Jim.%20*Cottril,%20J.%20An%20Overview%-
   20of%20Theories%20of%20Learning.%202003.pdf

This is an essay found online by Jim Cottrill, who wrote this essay and used as part of his thesis in 1996. It is a brief essay describing theories of how people learn and how to teach math.

He presents theories from Piaget, Skinner, Vyotsky, Lakoff, and Nunez, but, with very significant message. He also discusses that the initial reference above: Theories of Mathematical Learning (1996) has improved application for preschool learning.

Each theorist has his own theories and how to use for the benefit of children/ students.

Thompson states: "Vinner's idea of concept image focuses on the coalescence of mental pictures into categories corresponding to conventional mathematical vocabulary, while the notion of image I've attempted to develop focuses on the dynamics of mental operations."

"Schoenfeld (1985) perceives a student's mathematical understanding as the ability to solve problems. He has identified four categories of knowledge which influence this ability. The first is resources, the student's foundation of basic mathematical knowledge. The student also needs heuristics which are a set of broad problem-solving techniques. Third is control over the resources, i.e., whether or not a student selects necessary resources. Finally, the student brings belief systems to bear on the problem situation. All four of these categories must be taken into account when explaining a student's behavior in mathematics."

All theorists use highly intellectual language, but they all sound familiar to what has already been discussed: Mental pictures, mental operations, and broad problem-solving techniques.

8. ***What's Math Got to Do with It?*** Book by: Jo Boaler; Viking Publishers, 2006.

Ms Boaler is a prior professor of mathematics at Stanford Universtiy, and currently Marie Curie Professor of Mathematics Education at the Univesity of Sussex in England. She discusses some research, reasons for poor performance in the mathematics classes, and solutions to improve math education. It is well written and easy to follow. I will provide some general concepts and ideas from the book. However, it is recommended for additional reading.

She presents the problems that exist in numbers and math education in this country. She states that students are forced to learn in a certain, structured way. They learn in silence, without any interaction or discussion; while their teachers are trying to "show" them what they are supposed to do, often in a very uninteresting way.

Her solutions include: Allow students to explore their own best way to learn. Teachers should allow open discussion and encourage expression by the students in the class room. Give different ways to do a problem, and encourage them to explore different methods to accomplish math problems. Find more fun ways to utilize math and incorporate into their everyday lives. Give real life examples of math problems.

An excellent quote from her book is: "The very best way to teach children helpful strategies is to provide interesting settings, problems, and puzzles that require the strategies and then to share and discuss successful methods and strategies at frequent intervals. It can also be valuable to teach students mathematical strategies more directly, and over a short space of tie, as we did in the summer school teaching dexribed in the previus chapter." (p193)

She frequently recommends "puzzles", however doesn't mention "games" or "boardgames". Being British, she may have meant "puzzles" as possibly other games. But the idea is to stimulate the mind without rote memorization.

I couldn't agree more. Many of the concepts she presents are what I have presented above and ***Nelson's Train Stops*** certainly fills her requirement for "puzzles" to promote numbers and math learning.

9. Why Teaching Number Principles in Kindergarten Is Important: Elementary Math; Subhah Agarwal, A Math Expert; You tube Video: https://www.youtube.com/watch?v=5rzFsBulDX0

A very short video on why it is important to teach "number principles" in kindergarten. She says she is a "Math Expert", even though visually a very young expert. I couldn't find her background or credentials and therefore why she considers herself a math expert.

However, she gives a short but excellent explanation of why a child needs to learn "principles" and "relations" of numbers and "what they mean". In fact, she may say "why" better than I have tried above. However, it is totally in cinque with what I presented above. Since it is so short, and said so well, I transcribed her working exactly:

"Hi, my name is Subhah Agarwal, and I'm a math expert. And today, we are going to go over why teaching number priniples in kindergarten is important. So, number principles just means: understanding relations and meaning of numbers. So understanding, for example, that 5 is less than 6 or what 5 apples mean, like 5 physical apples. The reason we want to learn this, is because it is going to form the foundation for future mathematics, like addition, subtraction, multiplication, division. All of that is going to depend on us being able to understand what numbers are and what they mean. This is really important in their ability to do math in the future. Because understanding what a number is and what it means makes the difference between a kid struggling and trying to memorize this big abstract set of rules or actually being able to reason and understand and apply the math to everyday life. And building a foundation for a future interest. My name is Subhal Agarwal, and thank you for taking an interest in math."

This is very well said. She also presents many other math education videos that are very straight forward and easy to understand.

10. Kyle, Caroline; PhD in Education: You Tube Video: YouTube: https://www.youtube.com/watch?v=STrE2w-p0g0

Ms. Kyle teaches a visual "card" of each number. She has several different videos. I don't see what her background or qualifications are.

She teaches a card called: a 10 frame. Then she fills in a certain number of frames and then presents to the child so the child develops a "visual" of the card for each number: 1-10.

For any number 5 or larger, she teaches the child to fill up the 5 on one side first. Therefore, the child is able to use the principle of 5's and 10's. For example 6 has 6 frames filled in. She finds that children using these cards are more engaged than children that are working with "Worksheets" which they find very uninteresting.

Her video also shows that there is lots of interaction between her and the child, obviously a very important aspect. She finds that students hate math by the time they reach second grade. They need to be shown that it is not dull and boring, but vivid and alive.

This appears to show that using a tool or game that allows the student to do something manual while doing problems is more effective. This is very similar to my philosophy and my interactive math game: *"Nelson's Train Stops"*.

You Tube: As you might guess, there are thousands of math education videos online. This should be a great tool for young people to hear certain topics over and over to make sure they get it down, especially if they are struggling with a certain topic or aspect. Other uses of technology should also be appealing to them and encouraged.

11. Teaching Math to People Who Think They Hate It; Online Article; The Atlantic;
http://www.theatlantic.com/education/archive/2014/10/teaching-math-to-people-who-think-they-hate-it/381125/

This is an article I found online. A popular Cornell professor, Steven Strogatz, author, columnist, and Professor of Applied Mathematics at Cornell University, tries to help "language-arts types" learn how to "make math" instead of just studying it. Strogatz believes the key to (teaching liberal arts majors) lies not in the material, or the inherent talent of the student, but in changing the way math is taught to liberal arts majors.

The curriculum he teaches is called Discovering the Art of Mathematics: Mathematical Inquiry in the Liberal Arts (DAoM); it was developed at

Westfield State University by Julian Fleron and three colleagues and funded by a grant by the National Science Foundation. The DAoM approach, which is publicly available through a free collection of books and workshops, is rooted in inquiry-based learning: It focuses on student-led investigations into problems, experiments, and prompts. The typical mathematics for liberal arts class on the other hand, is typically presented in lecture format, usually by non-tenure track instructors, and only serves to further disenfranchise students, Fleron claims.

In an email sent after his first week of class, Strogatz described what this vision looks like when implemented in the university classroom. Using an exercise from the DAoM book *Games and Puzzles*, Strogatz handed each of his students a pair of scissors, as well as a piece of paper with a scalene triangle drawn in the middle of it. (A scalene triangle is one in which all three sides are different lengths.) He then challenged them to cut out the triangle using only a single straight cut. When they looked baffled, Strogatz told them they could fold the paper any way they pleased before cutting it.

Strogatz himself admits that he had trouble the first time he played around with the exercise. At the end of class, Strogatz asked the students if they wanted a hint, but they shouted him down, refusing his help. He stated:

"They were having a true mathematical moment. That is, they were deeply engaged with a puzzle that made sense to them, and they were enjoying the struggle. They were feeling what anyone who loves math feels, the pleasure of thinking, and the pleasure of wrestling with a problem that fascinates. I told the students to think about the scalene triangle over the weekend and to try it in their dorm room. Over the weekend I started to get emails from some of them, expressing the excitement they felt when they solved it."

He then goes on to say: "If we only teach conceptual approaches to math without developing skill at actually solving math problems, students will feel weak. Their mathematical powers will be flimsy. And if they don't memorize anything, if they don't know the basic facts of addition and multiplication or, later, geometry or still later, calculus, it becomes impossible for them to be creative. It's like in music. You need to have technique before you can create a composition of your own. But if all we do is teach technique, no one will want to play music at all."

Very well said and totally consistent with what I have written above.

12. A Fun Way to Slide Children Into Math, Article by: Eddy Ramirez, US News and World Report, Posted May 8, 2008.
http://www.usnews.com/education/
articles/2008/05/08/a-fun-way-to-slide-children-into-math

This is a news report of a research study published in a prominent journal: ***Child Developement.*** Playing board games can turn your child into a math whiz. Disadvantaged children tend to lag behind affluent students in math, when they start school.

124 preschoolers in the federal Head Start program used a board game with a spinner and took turns moving pieces along a row of numbered squares. They played four times, for 15 to 20 minutes each session, over just a two-week period. Given even this short period of time, improved the childrens perspective and understanding of numbers.

"Parents and preschool teachers should know that playing number board games increases young children's numerical understanding and lays a foundation for future learning of mathematics as well," says Carnegie Mellon Prof. Robert Siegler, co-atuher of the study.

This appears to have occurred without any guidance or instructions that occurs with ***"Nelson's Train Stops".*** Imagine what is possible with a game that actually shows perspectives and relationships and gives instructions on how to get the most out of such a game.

Reference: Ramani, GB, Siegler, RS, Promoting Brod and Stable Improvements in Low-Income Children's Numerical Knowledge Through Playing Number Board Games; Child Development 79 (2), pp 375-394, Mar/Apr 2008.

APPENDIX D

Numbers Fun Facts

Name	number of zeros	groups of (3) zeros
Trillion	12	4 (1,000,000,000,000)
Quadrillion	15	5
Quintillion	18	6
Sextillion	21	7
Septillion	24	8
Octillion	27	9
Nonillion	30	10
Decillion	33	11
Undecillion	36	12
Duodecillion	39	13
Tredecillion	42	14
Quatttuor-decillion	45	15
Quindecillion	48	16
Sexdecillion	51	17
Septen-decillion	54	18
Octodecillion	57	19
Novemdecillion	60	20
Vigintillion	63	21
Centillion	303	101

Googol: A googol, besides being the name of an internet search engine, (Google) is the name of a very large number. This number is 10 to the hundredth power. It is written with a 1 followed by 100 zeros. How big is this number? To get some feeling for its size, we will calculate some large numbers and see if they are as big as a googol.

A **googol** is the <u>large number</u> 10^{100}; that is, the <u>digit</u> 1 followed by 100 <u>zeroes</u>:

10,000,000,000,000,000,000,000,000,000,000,000,000,000,0
00,000,000,000,000,000,000,000,000,000,000,000,000,000,0
00,000,000,000,000,000

The term was coined in 1938[1] by 9-year-old Milton Sirotta, nephew of American <u>mathematician</u> <u>Edward Kasner</u>. Kasner popularised the concept in his 1940 book *Mathematics and the Imagination*. Other <u>names</u> for googol include **ten duotrigintillion** on the <u>short scale</u>, **ten thousand sexdecillion** on the <u>long scale</u>, or **ten sexdecilliard** on the <u>Peletier long scale</u>.

Google History: 1997

- Google.com is registered as a domain on September 15. The name—a play on the word "googol," a mathematical term for the number represented by the numeral 1 followed by 100 zeros—reflects Larry and Sergey's mission to organize a seemingly infinite amount of information on the web.

Measurements and Distance:
Millimeter - 1/1000th of a Meter
Centimeter - 1/100th of a Meter; Or 10 millimeters; equals abouve 0.4 inches.
Meter – 1 meter; equals about 39 inches or 1.1 yards.
Kilometer – 1000 meters; equals – 1.6 miles

Computer storage: memory and storage for computers use different terminology and may be confusing. You can use the same principles once you know the terminology.
Byte – 1 byte of computer storage
Kilobyte – 1000 bytes
Megabyte – 1000 kilobytes (or 1,000,000 bytes)

Gigabyte – 1000 Megabytes (mB); 1,000,000 kB; 1,000,000,000 Bytes (1 billion bytes)

Terrabyte – 1000 Gigabytes (GB); 1,000,000 mB; 1,000,000,000 kB; 1,000,000,000,000 bytes. (1 trillion bytes).

CD – holds approximately 600 mB (megabytes) of storage space.

DVD – holds several gigabytes (GB), depending on the version and generation.

(Above is for Disk storage. Processor and Virtual storage varies slightly)

SUMMARY OF APPENDIX
AND FINAL STATEMENT

I believe this presents to the motivated reader a wide range of different types of references. Many appear to be written for the academic and educational community and their ability to understand and utilize the information. I did my best to summarize the information for you here. However, I did have some difficulty interpreting how best they could be turned into usable information and action points.

I enjoyed doing this research and would encourage anyone with even a moderate interest, to review the above in more detail to see the extensive work being done in the name of teaching children math. I did not do much reasearch prior to writing the remainder of the book. My goal was to present how I approached numbers and math and hope it would be helpful to the reader.

Ironically, even with little prior research, I found that my approach to be very consistent with what is being discovered and promoted by highly important researchers and educators.

Hopefully, all of this will help all of you and your children.

DEDICATION

This book is dedicated to all of my family. First to my late parents who passed away much too early (Rosemary, age 47, and John Nelson, age 67) and were the reason I was so academically inclined and helped establish a loving atmosphere for learning. Then to my loving wife, who supports me in my profession, jobs, and various "projects"; and my amazing daughters for their motivation for themselves and me, as they are both very successful (CPA and attorney) and has allowed me to learn from them. Then to my siblings: Richard who passed away suddenly at age 59, but also wrote a book (***How to Prevent the Collapse of American in the 21st Century***), and a board game; Cynthia, who is 3 years younger and a certified teacher, who initially identified my unique perspective and gave me support in presenting my ideas; and Stanley, who is 6 years younger, and after many years returned to school to finish his Bachelors, then Masters degrees. All were very supportive and a motivation for me.

****

Figure 1: Basic Concept of "My Pattern"

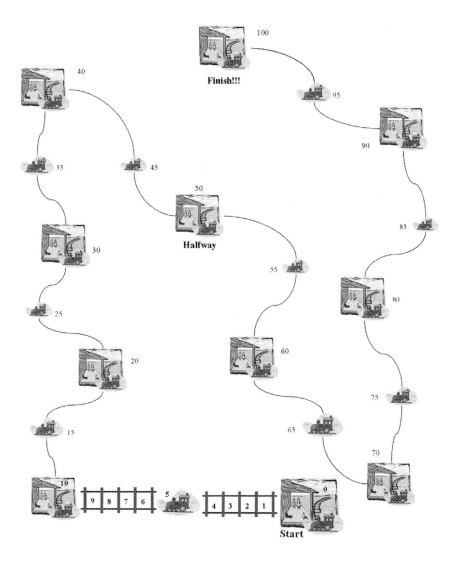

Figure 2 : How "My Pattern" Used to 200

200

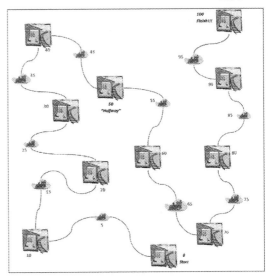

100

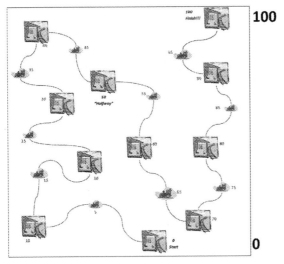

0

Figure 3: Using "My Pattern" to 400

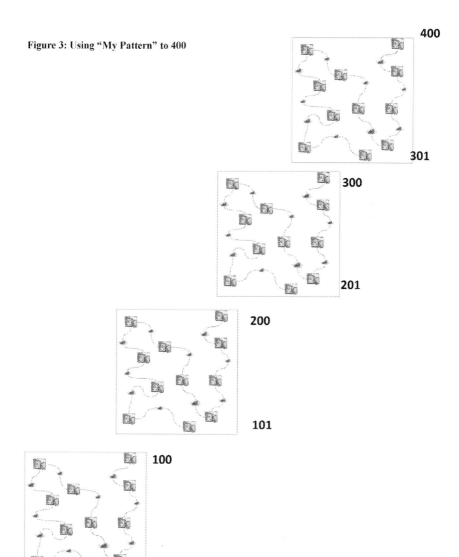

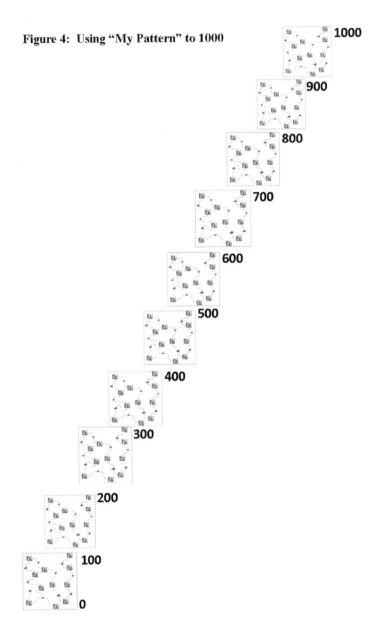

Figure 4: Using "My Pattern" to 1000

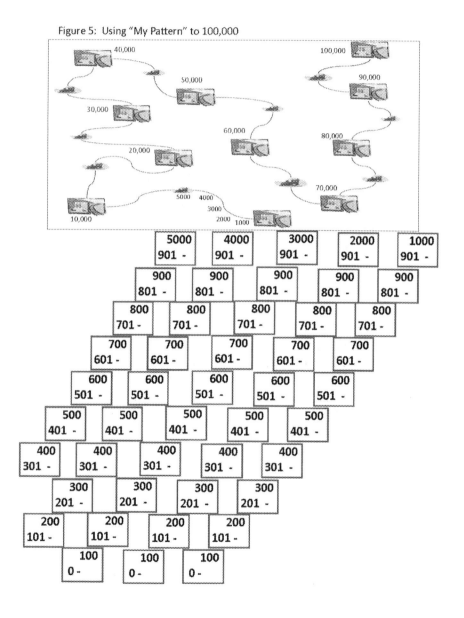

Figure 5: Using "My Pattern" to 100,000

ABOUT THE AUTHOR

Cary N. Schneider, DO, MPH, RPh grew up in Northwest Missouri, graduating from Savannah High School. He was an Eagle Scout, active in church, and was a tennis standout. He attended the University of Missouri, Columbia for 2 years, then transferred to the University of Missouri-Kansas City School of Pharmacy where he graduated with a Bachelors of Science in Pharmacy. After several years as a Hospital Pharmacist, he went on to medical school at the Kansas City University, College of Osteopathic Medicine. He initially worked as a rural Family Physician, then returned to residency in Emergency Medicine in Chicago. He has worked as an Emergency Physician for 20 years, most recently, part time. He also attended a graduate program at the University of Texas, School of Public Health in Dallas, where he earned a Master Degree in Public Health. He then worked as a Medical Director for Blue Cross Blue Shield of Texas for ten years, and recently retired. This has allowed him to work on projects such as this book and **Nelson's Train Stops** board game. He currently lives in Dallas, Texas with his wife, Laura, of 36 years. He has two daughters; one who is a CPA and graduate of the University of Notre Dame undergraduate and with a Master in Accountancy; and the other an attorney who graduated from the University of Missouri and the St. Mary's University (San Antonio, TX) Law School.

Be sure to visit the website: www.nelsonstrainstops.com

Printed in the United States
By Bookmasters